SEEING WITH THE HEART

SEEING WITH THE HEART

a spiritual resource

DR. ROBERT L. VEON

authorHOUSE®

AuthorHouse™ LLC
1663 Liberty Drive
Bloomington, IN 47403
www.authorhouse.com
Phone: 1-800-839-8640

Scripture quotations are from the Revised Standard Version of the Bible, copyright © 1946, 1952, and 1971 the Division of Christian Education of the National Council of the Churches of Christ in the United States of America. Used by permission. All rights reserved.

The photo for the front cover is used with the kind permission of the Forestry Society of Maine.

The photo for the back cover was graciously provided by Mike Lange of the Piscataquis Observer.

If any contributors or source materials related to this volume have not been properly cited, the author requests your forbearance. Omissions will be rectified in forthcoming editions.

Published by AuthorHouse   03/06/2014

ISBN: 978-1-4918-5453-2 (sc)
ISBN: 978-1-4918-5452-5 (e)

Library of Congress Control Number: 2014902978

Any people depicted in stock imagery provided by Thinkstock are models, and such images are being used for illustrative purposes only.
Certain stock imagery © Thinkstock.

This book is printed on acid-free paper.

Because of the dynamic nature of the Internet, any web addresses or links contained in this book may have changed since publication and may no longer be valid. The views expressed in this work are solely those of the author and do not necessarily reflect the views of the publisher, and the publisher hereby disclaims any responsibility for them.

Dedication

It is my pleasure to dedicate this book to my wife, Susan Jean Michel-Veon for her steadfast support and love through the years. She is my *sine qua non* and best friend. I will always be grateful for the way she has taught me to see with the heart and that "What is essential is invisible to the eye."

I would also like to dedicate the premise and perspective of this book to our grandchildren, in the hope that they will early learn and long remember what it means to be seeing with the heart.

Greer Ellen Veon
John Thompson Veon
Joshua Scott Veon
Alexander Samuel Nyiri
Jessica Lynn Veon

"'And now here is my secret, a very simple secret,' said the fox. 'It is only with the heart that one can see rightly; what is essential is invisible to the eye.'"

Antoine de Saint-Exupéry
The Little Prince

There's a beauty so delicate it will not be
captured or contained in canisters of words
for easy storage or transportation,
yet you can hold onto it forever
and take it wherever you go.

This awesome wonder of being
is seen only through the heart, where
perceiving its indescribable beauty
and reality of breathtaking magnitude,
one can only remain silent and weep.

Thank You, God, for a gift so rare
as grace, sculptured in my soul,
to enrich a heart like mine
when I perceive You through its lens.

I cannot stop thanking You beyond tears
for finding me worthy of Your love.

In Jesus' name. Amen.

Contents

Foreword

Some people are born to preach!

One such individual is Dr. Robert L. Veon.

In God's providence, both Bob and I (in my case, a number of years before) were led to become theological students at Pittsburgh Seminary. There, among many benefits, solid foundational work in the area of homiletics, the art and science of preaching, took place.

In addition to class instruction, each student was required to preach annually on an assigned text, without notes, before the professors and student body. The exercise was called "The Faculty Sermon." The label was truly appropriate, for when your homily was finished one member of the faculty (not announced in advance but who had earlier been provided a copy of your manuscript) delivered a response, accurately referred to as "The Faculty Criticism." When the experience at last concluded, you dusted yourself off, having been duly humbled, found comfort furnished by fellow students still awaiting their own ordeal, and moved on.

Naturally, each year of seminary the bar was raised homiletically. But the end result was that by graduation you had been strongly equipped for the many years of "pulpiteering" that lay ahead. Bob and I agree that the Pittsburgh style of training seminarians to be faithful and fruitful heralds of the gospel, for which we will be forever grateful, was indeed outstanding.

When asked, "And what is your profession?" many of the clergy are quick to respond "Minister." A lesser number dare to say "Preacher."

I am of the conviction that Bob Veon would prefer the latter designation. See if you don't agree as you proceed to read, reflect on and profit from his sermons, which follow.

—*Robert L. Kelley, Jr., DD, PhD*
Prof. Emeritus, Pittsburgh Theological Seminary

Preface

I am privileged to have had professors and role models of preaching that I consider to be among the best in the world: H. Ray Shear, DD, Frederick Bruce Speakman, DD, and Robert L. Kelley, PhD, DD, of Pittsburgh Theological Seminary; James S. Stewart, DD, of the University of Edinburgh, Scotland; and Raymond E. Brown, SS, PhD, of Union Theological Seminary in New York City.

H. Ray Shear was always immaculately and properly dressed. He expected his students to be clothed appropriately as they prepared to enter their profession. Not surprisingly, he taught that preaching should be neat and uniform in construction. The biblical passage under consideration was to have been prayed over and thoroughly prospected by the neophyte preacher, who he promised would then find the jewels in the text and be able to share them. He held that preaching should be sound, strong, and succinct in order to hold the listener's attention. Structure and sequence were stressed. He insisted on a powerful introduction, which signaled what was to be said to the listeners. This was to be followed by three distinct and biblically consistent sections defining and illustrating the premise. The final paragraph was to bring it all together with a conclusive summary. I am indebted to Dr. Shear for these formative teachings.

Fred Speakman had a style of preaching that was more like storytelling. I recall that he engaged our ability to write descriptively by having us imagine pausing on the way home from school on a warm, sunny day in the fall of the year, sitting on one of those stainless steel stools with a faded red seat at the soda fountain of the local drug store, having just finished a strawberry ice cream soda, slowly stirring and tapping the remaining little clusters of bubbles at the bottom of a tall, old-fashioned, ice cream soda glass. Given such a richly detailed narration, a reader could picture himself or herself sitting on the very next stool. In light of that example, we were instructed to visualize standing beside Jesus as He taught His disciples along the shores of the Galilean Sea. Our task was, and still is, to describe the scene in such vivid detail that the readers can see, hear, and feel it unfolding before them.

Robert Kelley, who in his undergraduate years was a cheerleader at the University of Pittsburgh, taught us that preaching should be exciting! We learned to catch the attention of our listeners by telling them of the enthusiasm that Jesus had when teaching the Truth. I am grateful to him for inspiring me to be clear, concise, compelling, Christ-centered, and convincing. He had a genius for alliterative outlines that, in conjunction with head-turning, eye-popping subjects, can make a sermon unforgettable. He taught us to engage in exegesis, the study of scripture, energetically! Which of us can forget the first week of school, when he jumped around the front of the classroom, teaching the Greek alphabet as if it were a cheer. I am grateful that he taught me to be a cheerleader for the Lord!

James Stewart, one of the greatest preachers of the English-speaking world in the last century, taught that teaching should be proclamation! I had the privilege of doing one year of post-graduate study under him at the University of Edinburgh in Scotland. He professed that the preacher has been given the opportunity to passionately proclaim the Lordship of Jesus Christ and the wonderful grace of God.

Raymond Brown, under whose guidance I studied the Gospel of John in the early 1990s, taught me the value and necessity of scholarship and the search for Truth, no matter how busy and complicated parish life could be. His love of John's gospel made his preaching as moving as his teaching and writing. He taught me to study, study, study and then study some more, since there is always more to learn. John has been my friend for life and will be in eternity.

From these teachers of mine I have learned many things. They taught me that the most important concepts of preaching are:

> A Pattern—H. Ray Shear
> A Picture—Frederick Bruce Speakman
> A Passion—Robert L. Kelley
> A Proclamation—James S. Stewart
> A Precision—Raymond E. Brown, SS

Acknowledgments

Any book is a cooperative undertaking and project. I would like to express my gratitude to all who have been a part of this book's conception and development.

I owe a very special debt to all of the members of my congregations who have heard these sermons and responded so graciously to them. For fifty years, these individuals have listened patiently and helped me develop and hone my skills as a preacher. Their commendations, criticisms and suggestions have shaped my journey of communicating the Gospel of Truth year in and year out.

Particular thanks goes to the Rockwood Community Church in Rockwood, Maine, for generously seeing that this volume would finally be made available. This quant log chapel on the western shore of Moosehead Lake opens each Memorial Day weekend and remains open until the last Sunday in September. Thus, it is a seasonal ministry composed of "the locals" and people "from away," vacationers who come to enjoy the mountains, forests, and waters of the North Woods.

The Rockwood Community Church has historically been connected in ministry to the Union Church, UCC, of Greenville, Maine. These churches have an affiliation with the United Church of Christ, but are a place of worship for all people of faith from a variety of denominations.

The Union Church is open year-round, with an active parish program throughout the year. The response of this congregation to the preaching of these and other sermons has been a source of encouragement over the last ten years. The congregation has been instrumental in urging me to make this volume available.

I am very grateful for one of my students at Beal College, Linda Gagnon, who transformed the raw materials of sermons on cassette tapes into a manuscript.

A year-round resident in the village of Rockwood, Nancy Ayer is a school librarian and clerk for the church council at the Rockwood Chapel. She was influential in bringing these pages to life, by preparing the prototype of this volume.

This book may not have been published without the work of Martha Herrick, a Union Church member, who applied her exacting schoolmarm charm to at least two efforts of typing and proofreading, making the grammar tolerable and presentable.

I am indebted to another member of the Greenville congregation, Mary Cyr, who performed a labor of love by organizing, editing, re-typing and preparing this volume for publication. Without her effort, this book would have remained a number of extraneous manuscripts. I will always be grateful.

I also want to acknowledge my professor and friend, the late Dr. Robert L. Kelley, for writing the Foreword of this book. I will always remember one of my evaluations in the seminary chapel, when he was assigned to critique my preaching. He concluded his remarks by saying, "Veon keeps pinning ruffles on the stars." I regret that he predeceased this book's publication by a matter of mere months, denying me the privilege of presenting a copy to him.

I thank all of the people with whom I have studied, worked, and lived. They are all woven into, or helped in the weaving, of the words in this volume.

Your pastor, friend and student,

Dr. Robert L. Veon

Introduction

This book is a compilation of sermons, selected from over fifty years of preaching. They were intended to present the ancient stories of scripture in a manner that would allow the modern-day listener or reader to participate in them. When I delivered them, I wanted the folks sitting in the pews to see the scenes and know the people in them. After two trips to the Holy Land, I felt compelled to make my descriptions authentic.

I visited the quietly serene setting of the Jordan River, near Caesarea Philippi in Galilee, where Jesus once brought His disciples, after telling them to "Come aside with me and rest awhile." I felt like I had accompanied them on their sacred retreat.

Sitting among the ruins of the synagogue in Capernaum, the hometown of Peter, I could hear the gentle waves of the Galilean sea wash upon the shore. Jesus, who frequently visited Capernaum, may have sat in that very spot. I stood near one of the old pillars that once supported the roof of the synagogue, prayerfully imagining Jesus sitting inside it, being handed the scriptures from which He would teach.

At the edge of the Pool of Bethsaida, I waited for Him to say to me personally, as He had to the man who had been ill for thirty-eight years, "Get up and walk!"

On the second Sabbath of Easter, I sat on the stairway of the Upper Room in Jerusalem. On that same night many years before, the resurrected Christ appeared to the disciples. He walked directly to Thomas, "Doubting Thomas," and said to him, "Put your finger here, and see my hands; and put out your hand, and place it in my side; do not be faithless, but believing." Sitting there, I imagined Jesus walking up those stairs, pausing before me to confirm my faith in the reality of His resurrection. He was as alive to me as He had been to Thomas. "My Lord and my God!"

On and on, the places became ever more vibrant and vivid with the contemporaneous presence of the One who had lived there two thousand years ago. Enough said. As my editor would agree, that's for another volume.

One of the sermons in this collection, *I, Barabbas*, was preached in the early sixties to my first congregation, the First Presbyterian Church of Clarksville, Arkansas. It spurred the imagination of a student of the College of the Ozarks, who worshipped with us. Years later, he turned the sermon into a drama for his church in Texas.

That same sermon was delivered some thirty years later, at a memorial service for Dr. Fred Speakman at the Westminster Presbyterian Church in Dayton, Ohio, where I had served as interim senior pastor in the early nineties. The service was part of the church's 200th Anniversary Celebration. Mrs. Zoe Speakman, his widow, was grateful for the sermon, which was so reminiscent of her husband's preaching.

Between each sermon you will find a "prayer-poem," many of which were written for the then-weekly newsletters, while I was serving as Senior Pastor. These prayer-poems express my thoughts and feelings amidst the joys and satisfactions of a large church.

The resiliency of faith, shared among the members and staff of the congregations in which I have served, inspired the writings in this book. As we all know and sing in our hearts:

> He lives, He lives, Christ Jesus lives today!
> He walks with me and talks with me
> Along life's narrow way.
> He lives, He lives, salvation to impart!
> You ask me how I know He lives?
> He lives within my heart.

> *(He Lives,* Alfred H. Ackley*)*

In the moment of selfless abandonment
when the heart silently slips into surrender and
the soul yields to what it senses,
one experiences the absorbing surprising love of God.

After all is considered and calculated
against the cost of losing the longing self,
overcome by wonder and breathless ecstasy,
one finds oneself in the arms of a gracious Will.

When in that timeless moment while eternity waits
to do the impossible and the most beautiful,
it is fitting that the heart beats with a beat not its own
and sings, "I am the handmaiden of the Lord
may it be to me as you have said . . ."

My soul glorifies the Lord and my
spirit rejoices in God my Savior.

One's soul so surrendered and yielded
is now prepared to hold the meaning of Christmas Eve.

In Jesus' name. Amen.

I Remember the Night

And she gave birth to her first-born son and wrapped him in swaddling cloths, and laid him in a manger, because there was no place for them in the inn.
—Luke 2:7

The flame from a small open oil lamp flickers, causing shadows to fall, shimmering and dancing on the white wall behind an old man. He is sitting at a large wooden desk, counting coins and bagging money. It is the end of a busy day in a boarding house in Beersheba, the last major stop before the desert and the main road to Egypt, beyond the hill country of Judea. One hour after closing time, old Eliab slowly gets up from his chair as his wife, Rebecca, brings him word that a distinguished visitor from Jerusalem awaits him at the door.

"Come in, come in! Welcome to the most hospitable inn between Jerusalem and Alexandria. Join me here in my den, where I've been closing my books for the day. Sit here by the light, so I can see you. Rebecca tells me your name is Luke, that you're a physician interested in research and writing. You've come this way searching for information, seeking answers about that night long ago in Bethlehem. Let me pour you a chalice of wine. You have traveled far, on this cold night.

"I have rarely spoken about it. That night was too intimate to be exposed, too sacred to be vulgarized by verbalizing it to those who didn't understand. Or even try to understand.

"I remember the night as though it were yesterday, even these many years hence. I am an old man now, soon to retire, contentedly waiting out my remaining days here, along this dusty road running across the desert. But I was young then, working at the inn in Bethlehem, which was owned by Rebecca's father. I was impressionable, eager to please and determined to succeed.

"We had only recently married and were deeply in love. It seemed as if we were spiritually synchronized. We could speak without words and be near each other even when apart. It was as though we breathed the same breath, shared the same heart and saw with the same pair of eyes. It was a precious time for us. We enjoyed every minute of it, even though it was terribly hectic.

"Caesar, you will remember, had called for a tax. Every man had to return to the city of his father for the census. Our inn had more guests than you can imagine! It was a thrilling time.

"At that point in our lives, we were trying to save some money. Rebecca and I were grateful for the help of our parents, but we wanted to have an inn of our own, like the one you are visiting this evening. For this reason, I was eagerly and enthusiastically meeting the needs of as many travelers as possible, as each hour brought us nearer our goal. Ironically, our good fortune was because of Caesar!

"Yes, I remember the night. The inn was filled to capacity. Guests were huddled in the halls. They were sleeping in the streets, reclining on the roof, bedding down behind the inn in makeshift tents. Stubborn camels and braying donkeys were tethered in the vacant lot east of the building. We had hired extra help to cook over open fires, to feed the festive guests.

"Toward the end of the day, a young peasant, about my age, came to the door seeking a room for himself and his wife. I started to send them away, but Rebecca noticed the woman's condition; she was great with child. Rebecca pulled me aside and whispered in my ear, suggesting the stable. At least they would be sheltered. Better to lie on a bed of straw than on the street.

"I showed them to the stable. It was dilapidated, dirty and drafty, but it had walls and a roof. I quickly returned to the inn, which held more pressing priorities and greater possibilities. I soon forgot about the couple in the stable. It's strange, isn't it, how we remember what we want to remember, take an interest in what we are interested? We seem to blot out the rest.

"Long after midnight, Rebecca stood over me in our room, gently shaking my shoulder to awaken me. I sat up on the side of the bed, with every nerve awake and alive. There was a soft smile on Rebecca's face that I will never forget. There was an excitement about her that magnified her natural beauty beyond explanation. I reached out to touch her lovely face with my hand, but she took it, tenderly pulling me from the bed and leading me from the room.

"Scurrying down the stairs, Rebecca reminded me of the young couple in the stable. Out of concern and feminine sensitivity, she had gone out to see if they needed anything. While I soundly slept, she had helped that young woman deliver a baby boy.

"Standing there, in the cold night air, I felt warm.

In the darkness, there was light. Luke, it was a light I had never seen before or since. The midnight sky was studded and splashed with the light of a thousand stars, all competing for a place of glory. One star stood out from the rest."

The resplendent star of which Eliab speaks was the finger of God, pointing to an event that divided history between the way it was and the way it could and should be, "when the wolf would dwell with the lamb; and the leopard would lie down with the kid; and the calf and the lion and the fatling together; and a little child would lead them;" (Isaiah 11:6) "when those who had walked in darkness would see a great light;" (Isaiah 9:2) "and the earth would be full of the knowledge of the Lord as the waters cover the sea." (Isaiah 11:9)

It is *kairos*, God's time. It is the fullness of time when eternity invades everyday. The light of that star caused men to look to the heavens, whence God had come to earth!

"Some of us had dared to wonder how it would be if Jehovah breathed His life into the dust, creating out of nothing all that could be. What if God were no longer aloof and afar, but came up close to us, so close that He was like us in every respect, walking our walk, talking our talk, knowing our temptations and torments and troubles? We believed that if Jehovah came that close to us, we would know how much He loves us. The knowledge of His love would then give us confidence to respond victoriously to the pressures and pain of our existence.

"I could not stop these thoughts from racing

through my mind, as Rebecca and I stood there in the darkness that night. She softly spoke of angels singing and shepherds running, a mother's deep prayer and a baby's low cry. I know, I know, Luke. It's a fantastic story. I have spoken about that night only a few times. My listeners become uneasy; they mock me and tease me.

"But you are not mocking my story. You're smiling as though you comprehend it; your face demonstrates your acceptance. Write it down, Luke. Write it down. The world is looking for a new way, a new truth."

The story that Eliab told Luke was only the beginning; it ushered in the dawn of a new covenant. It anticipated a morning called "Easter."

Luke has heard about a supper in Jerusalem, Jesus' last supper with the disciples. He took the bread in his hands, blessed it and broke it, saying, "This is my body, broken for you." (1 Corinthians 11:24) After they had supped, he took the cup and said, "This cup is a new covenant in my blood. For whenever you eat this bread and drink this cup, you proclaim the Lord's death until He comes." (1 Corinthians 11:26)

The flickering lamp goes out, but the room is not dark. Eliab, Rebecca, and Luke—just the three of them are there—but they are not alone.

Old Eliab rises to his feet and reaches for Rebecca's hand. The years melt away and seem as nothing. Their conversation has spanned the corridors of time, walking them through the halls of history, along the galleries of grace. This elderly couple is young again. They stand hand in hand, as they had that night, when they peered into the stable behind the inn.

Yes, it is Christmas. It happens every time. It makes us young again. Go gently to the manger, my friends, because He greets you with gentleness and grace. Stand silently in the vestibule of heaven. Peer in wonder and amazement at the stable scene. Stretch your soul on tiptoe, as you look into the baby's face. He wants you to come up close to Him, because He has come up close to you.

Go gently to the manger; come up close. You will find Him in an uncluttered moment of your busy day, in the laughter of children, the smile of an old man, the eyes of a friend and the touch of someone you love.

Go gently to the manger; come up close. You will find Him in your persistent pain, your lingering loneliness and your tender tear of self-pity.

Go gently to the manger; come up close. You will hear Him in the silence of one whose phone never rings, see Him in the eyes of a blind neighbor, talk to Him in the language of one who cannot speak.

He is in the emptiness of a beggar's purse, the brokenness of crushed hopes and the longing of lost love.

Yes, go gently and you will find His gentleness, which takes our darkness and gradually turns it to dawn, takes our coldness and warms it from within, takes our brokenness and makes us whole.

He takes our lives and gives them back to us better than they had ever been. You see, that's what Christmas is all about.

Remember the night. Go gently to the manger. For it is Emmanuel! Can you hear it? Can you see it? It's Christmas once again.

Amen and amen.

What was there about Joseph
         so masculine, gentle and true?
What made him such a good carpenter
         father, friend, companion and Jew?

He had such an affirmative influence
         on his firstborn son, Jesus,
modeling the godly lifestyle
         our Creator wants in each of us.

So it wasn't so unexpected,
         when looking for a meaningful name,
that Jesus called Yahweh, "Father,"
         making our relationship ne'er the same.

Just let me be like His father,
         loving, strong, capable and true,
that my children may see in their dad
         what Jesus saw in You.

In Jesus' name. Amen.

I, Joseph

Now the birth of Jesus Christ took place in this
way. When His mother Mary had been betrothed
to Joseph, before they came together, she was
found to be with child of the Holy Spirit.

—Matthew 1:18

"There are many things that are special about this season of the year. Christmas is the time when what could never be, is; what you had always hoped for is strangely possible.

"I have always wanted to tell my story. In many respects you already know the account, the details of which have accumulated over time. You know many of the dimensions and delights of His birth. You never tire of hearing about them. But you have never heard about how I saw it. You don't know what I experienced. Now I am able to see His advent from the perspective of heaven and eternity.

"I, Joseph, am the son of Jacob. I was born in Bethlehem, which means 'the house of bread.' It was the city of my father, and my grandfather, and our forefathers. Tradition claims that some of Bethlehem's trees can be traced back to the days of David, the king. It excites me to think that I may have eaten fruit from the same trees as he did.

"Bethlehem was a beautiful village. Square, white, sunbaked houses lined the narrow cobblestone streets.

The houses were neatly stacked side by side, up the slowly rising slopes. The slopes were surrounded by olive groves, whose trees with their gnarled, knotty trunks, seemed to stand and stretch from earth to sky. Beyond the trees, extending as far as the eye could see, were pastures of green grass, where shepherds watched their flocks by day and by night. It had been that way for centuries; David was a shepherd boy.

"Bethlehem was the perfect place to pasture sheep for the city of Jerusalem, which was only eight miles away. Many of the sheep were used for religious rituals, especially during Passover.

"Bethlehem was also known for its excellent craftsmen. The metal workers attracted people from the Holy City, who purchased highly polished artwork and ornamental accessories to wear with their finery and robes.

"In Bethlehem, my father established his carpentry shop. He was renowned for his skill. The products of his hands were prized by the wealthy residents of Jerusalem, who came to buy hand-carved utensils, and tables, chairs and other pieces of furniture of various designs and sizes."

"Yes, my father Jacob, a wood craftsman, was a man of great reputation. He had sensitivity that was reflected in his work. He could grip a board like a vise, or he could lightly finger it, as though the grains were delicate lace. He taught me to value a piece of wood by the texture, smell and fineness of its grain.

"He showed me that a man could be tough yet tender, strong yet sweet. He was passionate and patient, friendly and forbearing, gentle and graceful.

He demonstrated devotion to his God, his family, and his vocation, in that order.

"There is no question about my father's influence on me. His quiet impression on my life molded and prepared me for the day when I, too, would have the responsibility of fatherhood.

"No one would have thought that through a miraculous chain of events, I would become the earthly father to a heaven-sent Son. I, Joseph, would have a son under fascinating circumstances that would impact our lives for eternity. He also would be born in the village of Bethlehem.

"As I have said, Bethlehem had plenty of craftsmen of all kinds. When my father Jacob died, I decided to move some eighty miles north, to Nazareth, in the hill country of Galilee. Nazareth was a quiet and insignificant little village, nestled among the hills of lower Galilee, overlooking the plains of Israel. I set up a shop, using the tools and supplies I had inherited from my father.

"I worked hard. Before long, I developed quite a reputation for my trade, as my father had done. I became active in the community and the local life of the synagogue.

"There is a more human and intimate side to this story, in which I know you are interested. Allow me to share it:

"I will never forget that day. It overcame me like a bright Galilean dawn. I was sitting with some of the elders of the town near the village well, on one of those gentle spring evenings, so quiet and so lovely in the Galilean hills. I saw her, among a group of other young women, as they were returning from an early evening walk after their chores.

"I had known her family. I had often seen her with her friends in the spring of the year, skipping and dancing down the cobblestone streets, their arms overflowing with large bunches of wildflowers. Oh, I had seen her many times before, but never in this way.

"Mary was no longer a child; she was now a young woman with beautiful hair and a contagious smile. Her eyes were radiant as the stars and blue as a summer sky. My heart started skipping beats. Her loveliness caused a flash and a flush to come to my face. When she noticed me, our mutual attraction exceeded and exhausted vocabulary and imagination. Poets and artists have failed to recapture it with paint or words.

"Over the months that followed, Mary casually stopped by the shop to visit. Although there was no 'reason' for her to be there, perhaps there was 'rhyme.' She enjoyed the smell of wood. She had a creative nature. Being fourteen years old, she had a teenager's curiosity. She watched with interest as I formed and fitted fragments together to build a piece of furniture. Sometimes she wanted to help by sweeping up the sawdust and shavings or by straightening the shop at the end of the day.

"In time, I noticed that Mary and I communicated without saying a word. The moments we shared seemed heavenly, made in heaven. It could be said that she brought heaven into my life. I know you understand, for she brought heaven into your life, too. Being near her made me feel closer to God. I developed a new appreciation for the Psalmists' words: 'Deep is calling unto deep.' (Psalms 42:7)

"I loved Mary, as I had loved no one before, nor since. With the consent of her parents, she being of marrying age, we were betrothed. Betrothal was the custom in our time. Did you know that legal betrothal was more binding than your modern engagement? Back then betrothal could only be broken through divorce, a divorce based on unfaithfulness.

"Of course, in our case, unfaithfulness was unimaginable, given Mary's purity and our mutual devotion to the God of our fathers, the God of Abraham and Sara. Anxiety and disappointment began coursing through my soul like a swollen river, when I saw the stares and heard the whispers.

"The news that Mary was with child shocked and staggered me. I couldn't believe it; I wouldn't believe it; I didn't believe it! I think you can imagine the strangling, wrenching doubt, the persistent pain that traumatized and tormented my soul.

"Making matters worse, Mary had an unbelievable explanation. She spoke to me in confidence of conversations with an angel, of being the handmaiden of the Lord, the mother of the Messiah. In Nazareth? A young virgin from an insignificant little village? It was incredible. I thought it was a fantasy caused by her anxiety and stress.

"As a good Jew, I was faced with only two options. The first was to publicly divorce her on the grounds of unfaithfulness, which meant that she would be stoned to death as an adulteress. The second was to have the marriage contract set aside quietly, while Mary went off to have her baby and live elsewhere.

"Oh, yes, I still loved her, but my faith stipulated that I could not marry her, if there were any question of paternity. It would be wrong for me to marry her. Finally, I chose the second option, thinking her public shame might fade in time.

"At night as I lay in bed, my head throbbed with questions. My mind was too troubled and my heart too bruised to be comforted by sleep. I tossed and turned, hoping for a quick return of the morning.

"Then one night, I dreamt I had been wrestling with an angel, just as my grandfather's namesake, Jacob, had done. When I opened my eyes, I saw a messenger from God."

Is that not the way it works? When you have nowhere else to turn, no place to go, God comes to you. When you have exhausted all reason and resources, God comes through. Just when you are completely at wits' end, at the end of your tether, He comes to succor and to save. That, my friends, is how God serendipitously surprises us. That, my friends, is what theologians call "grace."

"In hindsight, I see that God had been working throughout my life, preparing me to become part of His plan. I, Joseph, began to yield to the Lord's will, as Mary had yielded herself to be His handmaiden. The two of us shared the remarkable secret of grace: *Earthly life is all about multiplying grace upon grace.* By submitting to Him, grace took our ordinary lives and made them extraordinary.

"Then came the decree. All men were required to return to the city of their fathers for a census. For me, that meant going to Bethlehem. Out of concern for her safety and comfort, I tried to dissuade her, but Mary insisted on going with me. I helped her onto the back of a donkey. With another one loaded with blankets and provisions, we began our trip to Bethlehem. It became a journey into providence. It was supposed to be that way. I can see it now.

"It wasn't easy. Bethlehem was eighty miles from Nazareth. The roads were rough, when there were roads. Generally, the terrain was unmarked and difficult. We had to go slowly, since Mary was great with child. The donkeys were surefooted, but still there was joggling and bumping. We stopped frequently to rest, for the journey was trying, even for someone as strong and healthy as I.

"We stopped one night, just a few miles from Bethlehem, to make camp. We could see Jerusalem, so important to our religious history, off in the distance. Her glowing lights brightened the heavens. A strange sensation unsettled the moment. I saw a shadow on Mary's face, as she surveyed the landscape. It was as if she already knew that God's plan for her baby would begin here, in Bethlehem, and end there, in Jerusalem.

"The next day, we traveled on to Bethlehem, across those pastures of baying sheep, through olive groves, and into the city. I had to find a place quickly for Mary to stretch out and rest. There was no room in any of the inns, because they were all overrun with people returning for the census. Finally, exhausted, we found a stable, an old cowshed behind one of the crowded inns.

"With my carpentry skills, I made a manger out of an old feed box and filled it with straw. When Mary gave birth to the baby, I helped her arrange Him in the manger, so He could sleep. We heard the enchanting sound of angels singing. We saw shepherds running.

Lambs, calves and baby donkeys from the barnyard encircled us, enticed by a natural curiosity. And I, Joseph, had the privilege of standing there, listening and watching it all.

"You know the story. You have heard it many times. Let it sink into the center of your soul and be born in you with renewed devotion.

"They tell me that I have been canonized. The name by which I am referred is 'Saint Joseph.' Others may call me that, but the most important coronation of my life was the birth of that baby boy. I taught Him what my father had taught me; I played with Him as my father had played with me. It thrilled me that, as a young rabbi, He helped others come closer to God by endearingly calling Him *Abba* . . . Father . . . Daddy. He was the first prophet in our great tradition to instruct us to pray, '*Our Father*, who art in heaven.' This to me is more precious than any canonization by the church, for I have been coroneted by the King Himself."

Amen and amen.

Bethlehem's Babe was

conceived in bewilderment
born in pain and suffering
arrived in a cold, hostile world
laid in an exposed cradle
housed in a vulnerable stable
visited by lambs, calves and donkeys
threatened by an uncertain government
nurtured by humble, peasant parents

The Christ Child remains today as He was then
  the Promise
      the Presence
         the Person
            the Power of God

for all who need Him and believe in Him
in every circumstance and situation of life.

He is Emmanuel.

In Jesus' name. Amen.

I Remember the Stable

And she gave birth to her first-born son and wrapped him in swaddling cloths, and laid him in a manger, because there was no place for them in the inn.

—Luke 2:7

"My name is Aaron; my occupation, a carpenter in the now-famous city of Nazareth, in Galilee. Luke didn't meet me when he went through this area, doing research for his writing project. I never felt the need to tell my story. But now, cardboard cutouts and make-believe characters have fogged the reality of that night to the extent that some claim it was a fabricated fantasy, a farce. Others treat it frivolously, or ignore it altogether.

"I, Aaron, worked in Joseph's shop. He was a good carpenter, gifted with the right touch that enabled him to make beautiful things. He had an eye for finding the perfect piece of wood. He had strong, calloused hands and a grip like a steel vise. He was any man's match in Nazareth. But today . . . just look at him. He's become a ceramic statuette in a candy-striped robe.

"Mary. Mary, his betrothed, was young, attractive and sweet. She immediately captured one's attention with her warm smile and pleasing personality. But her face on figurines is cold and impersonal; her eyes are staring into space. In life, she was always aware, attentive and alert.

"Wooden wise men, papier-mâché animals, and

a plastic baby in a cardboard stable fail miserably at telling the story. Joseph and Mary were real live people, like you and me.

"One afternoon at closing time, as I was sweeping away the last of the shavings and sawdust, Joseph noticed a Roman centurion from the window. He was nailing a decree from Caesar Augustus to the door of a building across the way. Joseph went out to read it. When he returned, he told Mary the sobering news. He had to go to Bethlehem, the city of his ancestors, to be enrolled in a new imperial census. I remember glancing up in time to see a frightened look steal across Mary's lovely face.

"At that time, Mary was about eight and a half months with child. In just a few days, she would need the care and company of her husband. But Joseph had to go to Bethlehem; it was a legal decree. Because she did not want to be left alone at such a critical time, she decided to go with him, although he tried to discourage her.

"Joseph asked me to accompany them, to assist with the journey. He knew the eighty miles from Nazareth of Galilee to Bethlehem of Judea would be long and difficult, siphoning the stamina of the strongest traveler, let alone a woman in Mary's condition.

"I, Aaron, led the mule carrying food and our few belongings. Joseph was able to focus on Mary's safety and comfort, as we traveled up hills, through valleys, over rocks and across gullies.

"By the end of our third day, Mary began to tire rapidly. With courage and resiliency she pressed onward, without a whimper, without a complaint. Her positive attitude encouraged Joseph and me as the days passed, but her face, full and flushed, could not conceal her discomfort.

"Our nation's great past became alive and palpable, as our route took us across the Plain of Esdraelon, for this was the land of the great prophetess, Deborah. We passed Jezreel, known for the abominations of Jezebel, then Gilboa, where Saul and his three sons died in battle. Crossing Samaria, we arrived in the hill-country of Judea, where we remembered the patriarchs of Shiloh and Bethel. Farther south, we went through Shechem, where Elijah performed his miracles. Suddenly, the city of Jerusalem lay before our eyes. As we scanned the high white towers stretched across her seven holy hills, our hearts filled with emotion.

"Just past Jerusalem, Mary began asking us to stop for occasional rests. The joggling and swaying of the mule were making her nauseous and uncomfortable. It was dark when we reached the valley. Looking up, we could see the city of Bethlehem, our destination, lighted and inviting. However, the most treacherous part of our trip was immediately before us. The gray limestone was slick, causing the mules to struggle going uphill. At one point, Mary had to walk, painfully pushing herself up the slope. At last, we reached the outskirts of the village.

"Joseph became noticeably excited. Here was the city of his fathers. For him, it was a homecoming, a reunion with his past. With our destination in sight, Joseph knew we would soon find relaxation and refreshment, shelter and sustenance, care and comfort.

"Entering the center of Bethlehem, we stumbled along the busy streets. The noisy, smelly crowds were not what we expected. Out of the packed inns spilled rowdy centurions and seductive waitresses. The revolting odor of hot grease and spicy foods polluted the air, making it sickening for worn, weary travelers such as we to breathe.

"Mary's condition was getting desperate. Joseph's anxiety and frustration began to rise, as at place after place we heard, 'Sorry, no room here. We've been full for days.' With hesitation and a degree of embarrassment, Joseph suggested an old stable he had seen behind one of the inns. It would buffer us from the offensive sights, sounds and smells of the narrow streets and alleyways. It would offer shelter from the winter winds that blew across the surrounding open pastures.

"Joseph asked the innkeeper for permission to use the stable. He greeted us with an air of impatient disgust. He shrugged his shoulder, tossed his sweaty head and sneered 'Go ahead, go to the stable.' He had more important guests to serve than these peasants from Nazareth. Later, we learned that the innkeeper's wife had noticed Mary's condition. She whispered in her husband's ear, urging him to offer them a place for the night.

"Oh yes, I remember the stable. It was dark, dank, drafty and dirty, but it would suffice. Tomorrow we would look for a warm, clean room for Mary. Joseph and I did not know that this stable for cows and beasts of burden would become the courtyard of a King. Even as Joseph gently lifted Mary down from the mule on which she rode, she was experiencing the pain of labor. Delivery was imminent.

"Friend, this is the stark story behind the glitter and gleam of your miniature stables with electric lights for stars. These are the facts behind your painted plastic shepherds and their cotton-ball sheep. There, in that filthy, flimsy stable, protected from the wintry winds only by stacks of straw, without benefit of bed, warm water or nurse, in the agonizing cries and excruciating pain of childbirth, the Promised One, the King of Kings, the Son of God was born.

"A dove from the loft cooed its cradle song, as its mate answered approvingly. The mules shifted their weight from one leg to another, dancing with excitement. A curious calf scampered through a loose board, to look with big blinking eyes into the manger. A pair of bleating lambs snuggled against the woolly warm belly of their mother.

> Away in a manger,
> no crib for His bed,
> the little Lord Jesus
> lay down his sweet head.
>
> The stars in the sky
> looked down where He lay,
> the little Lord Jesus,
> asleep on the hay.
>
> The cattle are lowing,
> the poor Baby wakes,
> but little Lord Jesus,
> no crying He makes.

"Yes, I remember the stable. I remember the Savior, who from His humble beginnings, began to fill the world with love and grace, as He continues to do tonight. The angels looked down in song; the animals knelt in praise;

the shepherds hastened in adoration. I remember the story of redemption that started in that empty stable."

This is the way God had planned it for ages untold. It was His way of completely identifying with us, making our faith so down-to-earth that we mortals could not miss it. Our God is a God who serendipitously surprises us again and again with His grace and love.

It happened here, in a forgotten stable, not in Caesar's halls or Herod's court. It was *kairos*, God's time, when He got His bearings in the nasty, noisy world that needed Him. Unannounced and unassuming, God came incognito, as it were, staying just long enough to work His ways in the lives of ordinary people, while writing indelibly on our hearts, chiseling into the marble pages of history, the truth of which John writes, "But to all who received him, who believed in his name, he gave power to become children of God; who were born, not of blood nor of the will of the flesh nor of the will of man, but of God. And the word became flesh and dwelt among us, full of grace and glory; we beheld His glory, glory as of the only Son from the father, full of grace and truth." (John 1:12-14)

The story is still being written today, as God records your response and mine in the empty places in our lives.

Won't you enter the stable tonight? The stable is the empty, neglected, tried-to-be-forgotten place in our hearts. Why not go there? Encounter the Savior. Embrace His story. Experience the transforming miracle of Christmas, as you exchange fear for faith, cowardice for courage, weakness for strength, defeat for victory, anxious restrictions for affirmative abandonment. There can be and there will be "peace on earth," when the Prince of Peace is welcomed into those fearful, faithless, empty places in our lives.

Come into the stable, so you will know this year, like never before, what is meant when someone says, "Merry Christmas."

Peace on Earth. Good will to all people.

Amen and amen.

> I know not how that Bethlehem's Babe
> Could in the Godhead be;
> I only know the Manger-Child
> Has brought God's life to me.

(*Our Christ,* Rev. Major Henry Webb Farrington)

You will see him when you least expect Him.

He will surprise you in the most unlikely place,
at the most unlikely time.
He may come in a sweet, warm thought
or in a deep, dark pain.
In a time of estrangement
or loneliness
or fear.
He may come when you are most bewildered
or befuddled
or lost.
He tugs at you in a crowd.
He comes to you in the unexpected words of a book.

He surprised people like you and me,
who had looked
pondered
anticipated and
waited for His coming
in the improbable setting of a forgotten stable,
filling our lives with joy beyond imagination and
description.

Who would have thought?

It's the Adventure of Advent!
So keep looking
pondering
anticipating and
waiting for His coming,
for as the poet reminds us:

"Closer is He than breathing,
and nearer than hands and feet."

(Alfred, Lord Tennyson)

Dr. Robert L. Veon
December 7, 2013

Silence sweeps across
the soul like a fresh breeze
scanning the uncharted depths of being
for the canyons of hidden meaning
yearning to be known and explored.

Silence comes like a shade
pulled to shut out the screaming
sounds of a full day's scurrying,
leaving only the luscious gift of
a quiet evening's restoration and recollection.

Silence is the heart's signal
to stretch the soul up to new heights and
down into the rich reservoir
of the inner life of grace and peace where I'm
compelled to be still and know that Thou art!

O Christ of solitude and serenity,
lead me to the shores of restful waters
shepherd me in pastures green
quiet me in Your strong, serene arms
save me from the clamor of a thousand concerns.

In Jesus' name. Amen.

At the Campfire

And in that region there were shepherds out in the field, keeping watch over their flocks by night.
—Luke 2:8

"Places I love come back to me like music,
Hush me and heal me when I am very tired."
—Sara Teasdale

"There is a place in my heart to which I return, to hush my hurrying mind. It comes back to me like music. I return year after year at the time of His birth, a time that seems to roll open the manuscript of my mind, permitting me the pleasure of reflection.

"I remember a quiet place, away from the city with its pushing people, corralled and crowded into the narrow streets at census time. It's a simple scene, this one. Maybe that's why it means so much to me.

"The place about which I speak is but a short distance beyond Bethlehem. It is quiet, unassuming and rather common. Come with me now to that place. Let me share what happened to make music of my memory, even these many years hence.

"I, Azor, with a few other shepherds and our lads, were watching over a flock of sheep. It was a winter's night. The frosty winds found openings through the cloaks we wore, so we huddled closely to the coals of the campfire. The flock was quiet at that hour; only occasionally did a sheep stir. Now and again, I heard the almost inaudible bleating of a young lamb, seeking refuge from the cold against the warmth of its woolly mother. Sometimes I felt the cool momentary touch of a snowflake on my cheek, as the dark sky spit soft white crystals down to the hard, frozen ground.

"We humble shepherds were unaware that to us, before anyone else, would be made the announcement that the hopes and fears of all the years were to be met in the neighboring village, the city of David, that very night.

"Why to us? Why would this long-expected declaration of God's arrival, this *kairos*, be made to poor shepherds, while a few miles away in Jerusalem slept religious leaders, with education, culture and sophistication? How odd for God to have chosen not the privileged, but the poor; not the intelligent, but the inarticulate; not scholars, but shepherds.

"We shepherds may not have been educated, but we yearned for freedom from the iron fist of Roman domination. We hungered to walk the streets of Judea, without the harassment of the swaggering, swearing soldiers of the Roman occupational forces.

"Though we did not express ourselves with the language and vocabulary of theologians, we were waiting with souls stretched on tiptoe for the Promised One, the 'Wonderful Counselor, the Mighty God, the Everlasting Father, the Prince of Peace.' (Isaiah 9:6)

"Why not to us? Perhaps God wanted to make His entrance and epiphany to the docile, unpretentious, unpresumptuous minds of simple, everyday people like you and me.

"Thus, choirs of angels came to us on that holiest

of nights, triumphantly delivering an invitation from a God who works in mysterious ways, His wonders to perform.

'Come and worship. Come and worship.
Worship Christ, the newborn King.'

"The heavens became still once more, although the music of the angels resonated in our hearts. That which had been written by the prophets had become reality.

"As you might imagine, we were astonished and amazed. We quickly gathered around the campfire. Almost in one voice, we said, 'Let us go over to Bethlehem and see this thing which has come to pass which the Lord has made known to us.' (Luke 2:15)

"Delirious with childlike enthusiasm and excitement, we took no time to debate or discuss the details. We hastened to confirm the angel's announcement with due speed. It was then that I, Azor, reminded the rest that someone needed to stay behind to tend the flock and the fire. Against their protestations, I said, 'I'm older; I will remain at camp. You go on ahead. The angel said, "He has come!" Look into His face for me. Now, be gone with you!'

"I remember how grateful they were. I could tell by the look on their faces. They left immediately, speedily stumbling down the hill, jumping over the brooks, leaping over the rocks, sprinting across the grassy pastures, entering the city gates, navigating the narrow cobblestone streets until, at last, they stood where the young child lay.

"As the stars looked down and the cattle lowed, a young mother had suffered the trials and torments of birth, bringing forth a baby boy, her first, strong and squirming in His bed of straw, in a flimsy, forgotten stable. She had benefit of neither nurses, nor white sheets, nor warm water; only an anxious, astonished father, awkwardly helping his wife with his calloused carpenter's hands.

"I, Azor, stirred the coals of the campfire and threw on another log, watching the momentary sparks of strawberry light spin up and about. The warmth was delightful. Alternately checking the fire and calming the flocks, I didn't have much time to think, focusing instead on the responsibilities at hand. Still, I wished I had gone, just for a moment, just for a quick glance at the Divine Babe.

"I'm an ordinary person like you. I felt a pang of pity for myself. I, too, had wanted to see Him. In fact, due to my age, I had yearned and waited longer than any of the others. A twinge of regret tightened my heart as I walked around the flock alone, on that desolate, windswept hill.

"Suddenly, it was as though another presence were walking alongside me. It was electrifying, emancipating. Gone were the biting cold and loneliness. Gone were my tight heart and self-pity. Why, I didn't even feel the lumpy stones under my feet, as I made those final rounds! In their place, I felt something big in my chest; a peaceful expansion and a growing, glowing liberation. I have felt it many times since, yet even now, I know not 'whence it comes or whither it goes.' (John 3:8)

"Soon, the others returned, competing with one another to tell me of the glorious night, of God who to earth came to dwell. Each told his story of wonder, assuring me he wished I had been there too. Finally, when the last had spoken, there was a long silence as we stared into the fire.

"You have had a private moment, haven't you, when time stands timeless, when you are so contented that you don't even move? You don't know whether you should smile, or sing, or wipe away the tear of joy that slowly streams down your cheek.

"Finally, someone kicked at the fire. As the flames brightened and rose higher, all eyes turned to me, awaiting my response to their accounts. But I, I could not speak. All they shared, I had already known. All they said, I had already heard. All they described, I had already seen. No, I could not speak. They later told me that when they looked at my face, they had seen a light as resplendent as that which had warmed the child's stable. I didn't get to go to Bethlehem, but Bethlehem had found its way to me, when I walked alone on that quiet hill."

If you can't go to God, God finds His way to you. It's Christmas! Emmanuel, "God is with us!"

Amen and amen.

You are God's gift
    to people for today
    friends near or far away;
    reach out to others needing to meet you.

You are God's distinction
    no one has ever been like you
    no one can ever own your uniqueness;
    you are now and forever a blessing.

You are God's potential
    planted in your head and heart is a promise
    of fantastic strengths and possibilities;
    you are a butterfly beyond the cocoon.

You are God's creation
    beautifully made, yet still in process
    developing, discovering, detailing
    the image of His grace and compelling love.

You are God's life
    a running, jumping, skipping,
    laughing, crying, singing reminder
    that for you "to live is Christ!"

Let go and live all He's made you to be!

In Jesus' name. Amen.

Dan, the Donkey Man

And all went to be enrolled, each to his own
city. And Joseph also went up from Galilee,
from the city of Nazareth, to Judea, to the
city of David, which is called Bethlehem.
—Luke 2:3

His name, 'Christ,' is not so much written,
but plowed into the history of the world.
—Ralph Waldo Emerson

"The apostles Matthew, Mark, Luke, John and Paul have recounted the story of His coming in eloquent, effective and exegetic terms. Because of their stature and credentials, you have rightfully listened attentively to what they had to say. Though it may seem presumptuous, tonight I, an ordinary workingman, would like to tell you the story as I saw it.

"A long time ago, I operated an old donkey stable in Nazareth of Galilee. The business had belonged to my father, but he was killed one night in a struggle with some of the occupational Roman soldiers. As the first-born son, I assumed care for my mother, brothers and sisters. This meant that I was responsible for managing the family business. I have been in that business ever since.

"My name is Dan. They called me 'Dan the Donkey Man,' with a snide smirk of sarcasm. You see, there was little need for donkeys in a village like Nazareth. Nestled as we were in the mountains of Galilee, the large marketplaces of trade and business were far away. There were few tourists, if any, in our area. Only infrequently did our townspeople travel any appreciable distance. So the people of Nazareth seldom had use for donkeys, or sellers of donkeys, like me.

"With business so slow, I often took long afternoon walks down the cobblestone street in front of the stable, which wove its slow way down the hill. After a block or two, I would cross the village square, go around the well, and visit my boyhood friend, Joseph, at his carpentry shop.

"Joseph was extremely well liked and had a fine reputation in the community. He was renowned for his craftsmanship. Unlike mine, his business was always steady. It seemed like every time I visited, someone was ordering a stool, a table or a chair. While I waited for him to finish with his customers, I tidied up His shop, sweeping away the sawdust and carrying it out back, where it was stored in a designated bin.

"From time to time we sat together on the stoop in front of the shop and talked. We reminisced about things we did in our youth, like fishing the Sea of Galilee or hiking in the golden hills. Often, our conversations worked their way around to serious topics, just as yours may sometimes do, when we least expected them to. During those talks, Joseph, who knew his Old Testament well, shared some of the great prophesies like: 'There shall come forth a shoot from the stem of Jesse' (Isaiah 11:1) and 'For unto us a child is born, unto us a son is given: and the government shall be upon his shoulder: and his name shall be called Wonderful Councilor, the Mighty God, the Everlasting Father, the Prince of Peace.' (Isaiah 9:6)

"Joseph was quite a man, you know. He was a good man; he was not merely a religious man, but authentically good. Everyone in the community looked up to him and admired his knowledge, wisdom, spiritual sensitivity and leadership. He was a good friend. When he heard others in town calling, 'There's Dan, the Donkey Man,' by simply placing his hand on my shoulder, Joseph boosted my patience and perseverance. Through his caring love of neighbor, Joseph taught me a lot about God.

"I remember it as though it were yesterday. One day when we were sitting on the door stoop, a Roman centurion came into the square. He announced that everyone would have to be enrolled for a tax in the city of his upbringing. For Joseph and me, that meant Bethlehem.

"This mandatory trip was inconvenient for Joseph, to say the least. Mary, his wife, was well over eight months with child. It normally took a week to travel to Jerusalem, then farther down to Bethlehem, but with Mary in her condition, it could take much longer. Out of concern for her safety and comfort, Joseph made a futile attempt to persuade Mary to stay in Nazareth, but she would hear none of it.

"Joseph was relieved when I offered to accompany them. With an expert donkey-handler like me along, he could give all his attention to his beloved Mary, while I guided and cared for the animals carrying our belongings.

"Going far up into the hills and across many miles of arid flatland with an expectant woman, we would need a considerable amount of provisions. It could be quite cold at that time of year, particularly at night, so we needed extra coverings and blankets for protection from wind and weather. I told Joseph that if he gathered our supplies, I would provide the donkeys to carry them. Thus, we started out on the long trek to Bethlehem.

"We crossed the Plain of Esdraelon, down through Samaria. We were thrilled to stop for rest and water at Shechem, which houses Jacob's Well, a symbol of our sacred past. Many years later, at that very same well, the baby in Mary's womb would be offered a drink by a Samaritan woman. Beyond Shechem, as we made our way up the hills and into the mountains, the travel became a little more difficult.

"I was glad I had chosen my most surefooted donkey to carry Mary. The barren rocky hills, carved by deep wadis and gullies, made the going rough. When the donkeys began to slip on those rocky paths, we slowed down or stopped to rest. We made our way carefully and cautiously, but determinedly, since we didn't want to be too far from a town, with Mary in the last days of her expectancy.

"When we finally cleared the top of the last mountain on the old road from Jericho, before our eyes laid Jerusalem, like a page out of a glorious book. Jerusalem, the Holy City, is a place of deep meaning for all Jewish people.

"Abraham, in obedience to God, came to this high place to sacrifice Isaac, his only son. Jerusalem is the home of our Holy Temple, which was planned by King David. Solomon, David's son, built it to his father's specifications. Not heeding the preaching and warnings of the prophets, the walls of Jerusalem were later destroyed and the temple desecrated, its leaders carried off into exile. Years later, Nehemiah and Ezra, with Jehovah's guidance, rebuilt the walls and restored the temple. Ezra called the people of Israel to revive their faith in Jehovah's promise of a king, a king who would lead his people into a better tomorrow, making all things new.

"We camped outside the city that night, so we could look across the valley and see the shining lights, suggesting a propitious presence, a Holy Other. We sat around the campfire talking and sharing our thoughts, but Mary seemed preoccupied. After awhile, we grew silent. Mary sat looking across the valley, into the city, with a sad expression on her face, as if she foresaw that what was soon to begin here would one day end on the very grounds upon which we sat.

"We left early the next morning, crossing over the valley and around the seven hills of Jerusalem. Soon we were on the road to Bethlehem. Our hearts ached when we stopped briefly at a lone bleak rock, erected to mark the resting place of Rachel. Later, a tomb would be built for her, which would seem to echo her wrenching cries for her children.

"The last night of our journey, we camped on the plain of Jordan, below the city of Bethlehem, which gently slopes upward, crowning the top of the mountain to the south. There, shepherds tended the sheep that gently grazed in the surrounding fields.

"In the morning, it was obvious that our time was getting short. It was difficult for Mary to get started. She had become very uncomfortable. I allowed Joseph and his young wife time to be alone with their whispered concerns. Joseph held her awhile, before tenderly lifting her to the back of my best donkey. I made certain she was balanced and secure, before slowly leading our small caravan toward the village.

"I cannot overstate the overwhelming disappointment of walking through the city gates of Bethlehem. We were immediately greeted by the acrid smell of burnt grease that saturated the air. The inns were packed to capacity, spilling wine-filled visitors onto the crowded streets. Peddlers were hawking tacky trinkets and wares. Spitting camels and braying donkeys were tethered in narrow alleyways strewn with animal droppings. The stench of the food; the intensity of the large milling crowds pushing, shoving and jostling one another; the noisy, frightened animals—all of it—made an unwelcoming climate for people like us, who had traveled so far. It was especially difficult for Mary, who by then was drooping over the back of the donkey's neck, in obvious pain. We needed to find lodging quickly.

"Joseph stopped at the first inn we saw. He entered the front door, while Mary and I waited at the street. 'No room!' was the response he received at that inn, then at a second, and at a third, and at every inn, time after time. 'No room!' Those words, accompanied by the slamming of doors in our faces, would resound in our ears unto the hallowed halls of history. 'No room!'

"Being the resourceful donkey man that I am, I began searching the area for temporary shelter, a place that others might have overlooked. I found an old neglected stable near the edge of the village, far from the village square, which offered privacy and protection. I hesitatingly suggested to Joseph that we should consider it. Reluctantly, he consented, because it was becoming clear that we had no other alternatives.

"I remember spreading a few piles of straw along the least dilapidated and drafty wall. I spread blankets over the straw for a makeshift bed. Joseph, with the hands of a carpenter, made a crib from a feedbox he had pried off the wall. After tying my animals near the open doorway, to somewhat buffer the bitter wind, I excused myself, leaving Joseph and Mary alone for the night, which would become the most special of all nights.

"I slipped out of the stable and headed toward the crowded village. It was so cold that I could hear the frosty grass crumple beneath my feet. After the stress of the day, I knew bread and wine would calm my mind and ease my heart. I went inside one of the inns to have something to eat and drink.

"After a couple of hours or so, I stepped outside to find the sky ablaze with light. The noise of the crowds had been replaced by music; the angelic song of 'Gloria!' rang through the night air. A bright and shining star pointed a long, graceful finger from heaven to the old stable, guiding the way for shepherds and revelers alike. I was astonished. That filthy, flimsy, forgotten stable standing in the shadows at the edge of Bethlehem, overlooked by all except a few weary travelers, had become the eternal center of the universe!

"I need not provide any further details; you know the story well, as you have heard it every year of your lives, whether you are eight or eighty. I am certain that no matter how many times you have heard the story, and indeed, have retold it yourself, it is still brand new, as it was that night.

"What you may not know, however, is that shortly

after the glorious event of Jesus' birth, the land became overcast by the dark clouds of paranoia, persecution and pain. King Herod, driven by a weakened mind and a group of irresponsible advisors whose jobs were at stake, sought to remove any challenge that threatened his right to be king. Because he had not found the princely babe born in Bethlehem that night, he sought to kill all male children under the age of two.

"Joseph, I now understand, was visited by an *angelos*, a messenger, who had warned him of the threat posed by Herod. He planned to take Mary and their baby to Egypt, until the danger had passed. He came to me saying 'Dan, I need two of your donkeys. I must take Mary and Jesus to Egypt, before the unthinkable happens. We will be leaving by nightfall.' I was delighted once again to meet the needs of my boyhood friend by providing the donkeys to carry his young family to their place of hope and safe haven.

"Throughout that day, Joseph hid his wife and their young son in a cave at the end of the village. Today, there is a chapel in that cave, maintained by Catholic priests. The walls are the color of pure white milk. It is said that while Mary was nursing her wee bairn before their long journey, droplets of milk fell on the floor and splashed onto the walls. When pilgrims stand in that chapel, the Holy Spirit paints it anew in their hearts.

"At nightfall, Joseph lifted Mary onto the back of my most sturdy donkey, the one that had carried her on the journey from Nazareth to Bethlehem only a few days earlier. He gently picked up his firstborn son, holding Him with the strong, steady hands of a carpenter. I watched, as with great affection, Joseph kissed his son's forehead and lovingly placed Him into

His mother's waiting arms. Joseph took the rope of the lead donkey out of my hand and embraced me quickly. Then they were on their way toward the land of Egypt.

"I decided to stay on in Bethlehem. Why should I go back to Nazareth? My best friends were no longer there; they were in Egyptland. The only ones left in Nazareth were those who had ridiculed my humble but necessary job, those who mocked and taunted me, calling me, 'Dan, the Donkey Man.' Business wasn't good there anyway, as you remember.

"Bethlehem, not far from Jerusalem, was on a thruway from Jerusalem to Egypt. It was a more promising place for me to develop a business that would put a few *shekels* in my pocket. The owner of the stable where Jesus was born sold it to me for a fair price. I renovated it and expanded it. That stable became the center of a whole new life for me in Bethlehem.

"I often think of what God said to Moses as he approached the burning bush: 'Put off your shoes from your feet, for the place on which you are standing is holy ground.' (Exodus 3:5) Believe me, friends, that stable had become a sacred place to me.

"Years later, I moved closer to Jerusalem, to the village of Bethany, which was an auspicious place to open an even larger stable. Being on the main road south, where all the caravans going northward would start, my business flourished.

"As the years passed, I lost track of Joseph, Mary and the baby. Oh, I heard second or third hand that they returned to the shop in Nazareth a few years later, after Herod's bloody scourge and death. Their family continued to grow. Joseph and Mary had a number of children after Jesus.

"Good Jews that they were, the family traveled to Jerusalem each year for the Passover. I recall hearing about one of their trips, when Jesus was about twelve years old. When the family was leaving for home, Joseph and Mary could not find Jesus. After a frantic search, they found Him in the Temple, asking questions that had been crowding His young mind. His questions left the priests and scholars baffled. Jesus was beginning to enter the age of accountability; He was discovering His own selfhood.

"His mother said to Him, 'Son, why have you treated us so? Behold, your father and I have been looking for you anxiously.' (Luke 2:48)

"In a manner that was strange for a child His age, He replied, 'How is it that you sought me? Did you not know that I must be in my Father's house?' (Luke 2:49) His reply caused his parents to consider issues mightier than themselves, issues that would change the thinking of the entire world.

"Jesus politely left with them and obeyed them thereafter. As your account records it, 'And he went down with them and came to Nazareth, and was obedient to them; and his mother kept all these things in her heart. Jesus increased in wisdom and in stature and in favor with God and man.' (Luke 2:51,52)

"Jesus enjoyed many years with His father. From him, He learned to memorize the Hebrew scripture and to sing the Psalms of the great King David. He listened with avid interest when His father told Him of the prophecy that a Messiah would come one day.

Together, they walked in the hills around Nazareth and fished a short distance away, on the waters of Galilee."

The two of them must have experienced many things together
      the skill with saw and wood
      the smell of woodchips and sawdust
      the quiet fishing trips on Galilee
      the walks along the vineyards
      the picnics in the pasture of sheep
      the nights sleeping under the stars
      the lessons from the Law and Prophets
      the tender times of teasing
      the hopes they held in trust
      the wrestling testing of masculinity
      the dependable, sweet, yet tough, love
      the genuine, uncluttered companionship
      the authentic openness and transparency
      the healthy love and respect for women
The relationship they shared was precious and whole
   Jesus and Joseph
      Father and Son.

"When Jesus was roughly the age of nineteen, Joseph, unfortunately, contracted an illness that led to his early death. Perhaps his lungs had been weakened, after a lifetime of inhaling wood dust. As the eldest son, Jesus became responsible for the family and His father's business, just as I had, following the death of my father. I later learned that Jesus left the shop, when His brother James was old enough to operate it. Jesus then became an itinerant rabbi, traveling the countryside preaching to the masses.

"One day, a compelling teacher came into Bethany with twelve of His students. They were on their way into Jerusalem to celebrate Passover. They stopped at my stable, because the young teacher wanted a donkey, upon which to ride the last leg of their journey into the Holy City. He seemed familiar to me, as though I had already known him. I don't know what came over me, but I gave him the donkey without charge, without obligation.

"As I followed behind them, I heard the crowds shouting 'Blessed is He who comes in the name of the Lord, Hosanna in the Highest!' (Matthew 21:9) Standing on spiritual tiptoes, I could see the people creating a royal entrance for Him. They were spreading their cloaks and palm branches over the walkway, cushioning His path, as He rode into the city upon my donkey.

"I saw the Roman authorities try to stop the celebration by approaching Jesus and commanding Him to silence the people, claiming that He did not have a permit for such a parade. I, Dan, heard Him reply that if the people were to become quiet, the very stones along the walkway would cry out.

"My friends, I am no longer, 'Dan, the Donkey Man.' People refer to me now with respect and honor. They call me Daniel, 'Daniel, Courier to the King!' Don't you see? It was my donkey that carried Him to the village of His princely birth; it was my donkey that carried Him to safety in Egypt as a newborn; it was my donkey that carried Him to the city of His kingly coronation, death, and resurrection.

"I am Daniel, Courier to the King, the King of Kings and the Lord of Lords. Alleluia!"

You are somebody special! You are God's child. He loves you as though you were the only one He had to love. In his gospel, the apostle John shares Jesus' clear and comforting words, "But to all who received Him, who believed in His name, He gave power to become the children of God." (John 1:12) The one who would become known as "Saint Paul," writes, "You who were once far off have been brought near in the blood of Christ." (Ephesians 2:13) Peter, the leader of the church and its first pope, reminds us, "Once you were no people, but now you are God's people. Once you had not received mercy, but now you have received mercy." (1 Peter 2:10)

You, my dear friends, are of infinite value and worth! For you, Jesus paid the price. He unexpectedly and miraculously enters into your everyday lives and changes them forever. You will never be the same again, for having loved Him.

Amen and amen.

Because You are such a surprising
God of enormous love and grace,
You permit me every once in awhile
to stumble onto a moment of spiritual perception.

These times leave me gasping in wordless wonder
and I once again become absolutely convinced
that You wish me to experience
Your incalculable richness.

You plan to include me and invest me
in a transforming glory and power,
animating my being with astonishing energy
empowering me to become who You hoped.

Thank You, God, for those glimpses of greatness
that focus me in faith once more
beyond all that I normally expect earlier
while filtering out immeasurable promise.

Keep me from trivializing my own becoming
remove all that pauperizes Your presence
stun me awake with unlimited possibilities,
while I bow before You in speechless awe.

Thank You.

In Jesus' name. Amen.

I, Matthew

*And after this He went out and saw a tax
collector, named Levi, sitting at the tax office;
and He said to him, 'Follow me.' And he left
everything and rose and followed Him.*
—Luke 5:27-28

The scene is a quiet study in the village of
Capernaum, late in the first century. An olive oil lamp
burns on a small desk, casting uneven shadows on walls
nearly hidden by the racks of scrolls that line the room.
The scrolls, written in Hebrew, are the result of years
of faithful effort by one called Levi. We know him as
Matthew. It is quiet. There is no noise except the old
worn pen scratching the papyrus and the occasional
shifting of Levi's feet on the stone floor beneath the
desk at which he sits, tirelessly copying a scroll, right
to left, right to left.

Suddenly, a rap on the door breaks the studious
spell. Levi, laying aside his pen, goes to the door to
welcome his guest. It is Josiam.

"So Josiam, you have come for scrolls to take to
the library in Alexandria. Join me at the table and let
me pour you a glass of wine. Josiam, in addition to a
vast oral tradition, there are many written accounts of
the Master's life.

"You are correct in assuming that Mark, who
traveled a great deal with our brothers Peter, Barnabas

and Paul, was the first to write about Him. Mark's account speaks with great enthusiasm of the exciting journey of the church's expansion.

"The disciple Luke also wrote about Him. Luke's account places considerable emphasis on the Master's miracles. Being a trained physician, Luke was interested in how and when Jesus healed the leper, calmed the demons, opened the eyes of the blind and straightened the limbs of the lame.

"Luke did much research while composing his gospel and his subsequent history of the church, The book of Acts. Acts is essentially a continuation of Luke's gospel. It is the second volume of the story he yearned to tell.

"My purpose in writing though, Josiam, is different than theirs. Though their accounts are valuable, Mark and Luke were not among Jesus' twelve original disciples, as I was. I, Matthew, was called personally to follow Him. I knew the strength and power of His personality. I knew His attraction, His winsomeness and His charisma. I knew the deep, manly tones of His voice and the clear sparkle of His eyes. I knew the grace of His spirit and the irresistible love of His heart.

"My purpose, the purpose to which I have devoted my days, is to provide the world with a collection of His writings and teachings. Just as the prophets of the Old Testament wrote, 'Thus saith the Lord,' I write that Jesus 'Opened his mouth and taught them saying . . .' (Matthew 5:2) Yes, I, Matthew spent more time with Him and heard more of His teachings than any of the others. 'Thus saith the Lord.'

"You know, Josiam, His teachings upset my life. Or I should say, they set it upright. They were unlike anything I had heard in the temple and synagogue. His words worked their way into my head and lodged in my heart. They gripped me in grace and would not let me go.

"The first time I heard Him speak, I stood at the far edge of the crowd. Hundreds had gathered to listen to Him, yet it was as though He spoke only to me, as though I were the only one present, an audience of one. I, Matthew, the tax collector, stood transfixed by every word He said.

"Later, after returning to my tax ledgers of lies, in my mind I could still hear his voice, speaking words like the ones on this scroll. I am calling it *The Sermon on the Mount:* 'Blessed are the poor in spirit, for theirs is the kingdom of heaven' (Matthew 5:3) and 'Blessed are the meek, for they shall inherit the earth.' (Matthew 5:5) Oh, I knew the words 'poor' and 'inheritance' in financial terms, but His interpretation challenged and tormented me.

"Look, Josiam, here He told us to love each other, even our enemies! I, Matthew, had loved little. I greedily used people for my own gain. I cheated and lied. I squeezed every *denarius* I could out of the citizens' purses. They hated me, but I hated them more. They were no more than filthy, foolish peasants to me. When I heard Jesus telling the multitudes to love their enemies, I laughed out loud! But days later, I wept.

"Then one day, Christ's shadow fell across my desk, blotting out my figures and calculations. His sweet words silenced the shouts of those who hated me. 'Levi—Levi,' He said, 'come follow Me.'

"Without a moment's hesitation, I left my tawdry

tax office to become His disciple. Here, Josiam, read this, and this line here. No, wait . . . just listen:

"'Do not lay up for yourselves treasures on earth where moth and rust consume, and where thieves break in and steal, but lay up for yourselves treasures in heaven, where neither moth nor rust consume and where thieves do not break in and steal. For where your treasure is, there will your heart be also.' (Matthew 6:19-21)

"'No one can serve two masters; for either he will hate the one and love the other or he will be devoted to one and despise the other. You cannot serve God and man. Therefore, I tell you, do not be anxious about your life, what you shall eat or what you shall drink, nor about your body, what you shall put on. Is not life more than food, and the body more than clothing? Look at the birds of the air; they neither sow nor reap nor gather into barns, and yet your heavenly Father feeds them. Are you not of more value than they? And which of you by being anxious can add one cubit to his span of life? And why are you anxious about clothing? Consider the lilies of the field, how they grow; they neither toil nor spin, yet I tell you, even Solomon in all his glory was not arrayed like one of these.' (Matthew 6: 24-29) 'Ask, and it will be given you; seek, and you will find; knock, and it will be opened to you.' (Matthew 7:7-8)

"'Everyone then who hears these words of mine and does them will be like a wise man who built his house upon rock; and the rain fell, and the floods came, and the winds blew and beat upon the house, but it did not fall, because it had been founded on the rock.' (Matthew 7:24-25)

"Is it any wonder that I have been changed, Josiam? Can you understand how these words have been fermenting in my mind and heart these many years?

"Yes, I am Levi, the tax collector, but I have become known as Matthew. I used to collect taxes, but now I distribute His teachings. I forfeited my position in society, but gained a promise of eternity. In losing my salary, I found my soul. When I discarded my colorful robes, I received righteousness, clothed and covered in grace. All this, Josiam, because *Christ saw beyond what I was to what I could yet become!*

"Jesus walks through the pages of my mind in kingly purple, Josiam. In writing my gospel, I have been spending much time tracing His family tree. I call Him 'the son of David' the King, attempting to show His direct lineage to the fathers of our faith.

"The prophets and psalmists wrote that all nations will come to Jerusalem to pay tribute to Him. 'Because of thy temple at Jerusalem kings bear gifts to thee.' (Psalms 68:29) 'Behold, you shall call nations that you know not; and nations that knew you not shall run to you.' (Isaiah 55:5) In my account, I pay homage to their words. I have Wise Men come from the east, looking for the new King.

"And as He was dying, Pilate mockingly tacked a sign saying, 'The King of the Jews' to His cross.

"I know without question that this King is enthroned in my life. He rules as King of my heart. He is the King of Kings and the Lord of Lords forever and ever! It is important for you to know, Josiam, that He is your King too! He can be your Savior, and the Savior of your

children, and the Savior of your world, if you will but
surrender and sing, with the ages yet unborn:

"Praise my soul, the King of heaven,
To His feet thy tribute bring;
Ransomed, healed, restored, forgiven,
Who, like me, His praise should sing?
Praise Him, praise Him, praise Him and praise Him
Praise the everlasting King!"

(*Praise, My Soul, the King of
Heaven,* Henry Francis Lyte)

If I could but touch Him,
Then all would be well.
My life would be whole again,
As others would tell.

I will reach out and touch Him
All the days of my life,
Sharing my experience,
Living above sickness and strife.

I will touch Him in the morning,
At noonday and night.
I will abide in His love
All the days of my life.

How can you live in grace?
How can you live in wholeness and joy?
Reach out to Jesus.
Touch Him and look in His face.
"And the things of earth will grow strangely dim
In the light of His glory and grace."

In Jesus' name. Amen.

A Miracle within a Miracle

Now when Jesus returned, the crowd welcomed
Him, for they were all waiting for Him. And
there came a man named Jarius, who was a
ruler of the synagogue; and falling at Jesus'
feet he besought Him to come to his house.
—Luke 8:40

And a woman who had had a flow of blood for twelve
years and could not be healed by anyone, came up
behind Him and touched the fringe of His garment.
—Luke 8:43

I am the master of my fate,
I am the captain of my soul.
—William Ernest Henley

The lines above, from the nineteenth-century poem
Invictus, express self-reliance, a quality that was as
esteemed then as it is today. A modern translation of this
sentiment is, "I don't need anything or anybody. I can
do it all myself, or I'll die trying." Sadly, we usually do.

Because we are human, we are not invincible,
although that may be difficult for us to admit. Rather,
we are fragile, capable of being broken under too much
stress. Our burdens are sometimes more than we can

bear. When we allow ourselves to reach out to someone, our loads can be lightened; our anxieties can be abated.

The gospel, "the good news," provides many examples of men and women who trust Jesus enough to bring their troubles to Him. The story I would like us to consider this morning is one in which He performs a miracle within a miracle. Two unrelated people in the same passage seek the assistance of Jesus, because they have nowhere else to turn.

"I am Jarius, a ruler of the Jews in the synagogue. My little girl, my only daughter, was very ill. She was dying. I had emptied my purse, sparing no expense, on the most respected physicians in the region, but none were able to cure her. My fear for her life was excruciating, exhausting.

"I had heard there was an itinerant preacher named Jesus, from Nazareth, in the mountains of Galilee. He was the uneducated son of a carpenter. Yet Nicodemus, a respected Pharisee of the Sanhedrin, sought Him for theological insight. They had an esoteric late-night discussion about being 'born again.'

"Jesus would talk to anyone, without regard to social status. Remarkably, He had a personal and profound discussion with a Samaritan woman with a questionable reputation. Remember, we Jews did not speak with unfamiliar women and had no association at all with Samaritans of either gender. Yet He spoke with candor to that woman about her private life.

"Jesus performed marvelous deeds for those who needed them most. One incident in particular was interesting and relevant to me. A nobleman approached Him in Cana, seeking a cure for his son, who was sick at their home in Capernaum. The man implored Him to go to his son before he died. Jesus said to him, 'Go. Your son will live.' (John 4:50) He cured the boy without even seeing him!

"Our great prophet, Isaiah, wrote that when the Messiah came, He would be called 'Wonderful Councilor, the Mighty God, the Everlasting Father, the Prince of Peace' (Isaiah 9:6) Excitement was growing among our people. We speculated that this preacher was the Messiah, our Savior, who would relieve today's suffering and give us hope for a better tomorrow.

"I had depleted all of my resources, subjecting my little girl to remedy after ineffective remedy. I, Jarius, was at the end of my tether of hope. Jesus was all I had left. Amid a crowd that had gathered to see Him, I, Jarius, reached out to Jesus."

Falling at His feet, Jarius besought Jesus to go to his house to cure his daughter. Seeing his distress and hearing the desperation in his voice, Jesus responded sensitively and affirmatively.

Hoping to witness a miracle, the crowd following them was growing; the emotional intensity was rising. Tightly packed, they were taking short, jolting steps. Elbow to elbow, shoulder to shoulder, they moved along the old city streets.

In the midst of one miracle, Luke begins to tell us of another. Within that dense crowd, a woman was suffering in solitude, isolated within her own worries. She was walking with her head down, trying to remain inconspicuous. She was being bumped and jostled about, as the human wave followed Jesus to Jarius' house.

We don't know very much about this woman. In his gospel, Luke calls her, rather brusquely, "the woman." Luke, whose writing is otherwise so descriptive and specific when recounting dramatic incidents in the Savior's ministry, omitted the woman's name.

Perhaps he hadn't known her name. It is possible that she was seldom seen in the marketplace or drawing water. She might have preferred to do her chores at odd hours, when few would notice her. Or perhaps Luke did not give us the woman's name, because he intended for us to insert our own. Who among us has never felt downhearted, defeated and desperate, like this needful soul?

"I am the unnamed woman. For twelve years I struggled with a personal affliction that had slowly drained away my life. I bled constantly. I was weak and anemic. Like Jarius, I had squandered my savings on physicians, none of whom could heal me.

"One might ask, I suppose, what I was doing in that crowd, being pushed and dragged along that dirty street. I, too, was hoping for a miracle . . . my own.

"Jesus was my only hope. But how could I, a frail woman in poor health, get His attention? I tried to get close to Him, close enough to touch Him on the shoulder. With every ounce of strength I had, I stretched as far as I could in His direction. I, an unnamed woman, reached out to Jesus."

Her fingers barely brushed the fringe of His robe. She quickly withdrew her hand, fearing she may have been too bold. Suddenly, the crowd stopped, knocking her to the gravel road.

The crowd stopped, not because they saw what she had done, but because Jesus had stopped. Turning around, He said, "Who was it that touched me?" (Luke 8:45) Peter, as only Peter could do, became irritated and impatient with Jesus. Urging Him to continue, he pointedly said, "Master, the multitudes surround You and press upon You!" (Luke 8:45)

Everyone denied having touched Him. Seeing that she could no longer remain hidden, the woman came forward, trembling. Falling down before Him, she explained to Jesus and to all present why she had touched Him, and how she had been healed immediately after doing so. He lifted her up from the ground and gently said to her, "Daughter, your faith has made you well; go in peace." (Luke 8:48)

That unnamed woman—Jesus called her "daughter." In times of desolation and despair, we all need to hear a kind word. "My loved one . . . go in peace."

When they resumed walking toward his house, Jarius received a message from one of his servants. His daughter had died. Upon hearing this sad report, Jesus reassured him, saying, "Do not fear; believe only and she shall be made whole." (Luke 8:50)

This story spiritually instructs us to reach out to Jesus, so that we may be made whole too.

Amen and amen.

Thank You, God,
  for Your precious gift of presence

      a beautiful moment
        so crystal clear
          radiantly peaceful
              soft, yet brilliantly bright

      when deep calleth unto deep
        being brushes being
          soul stretches soul
              heart hears heart

      a moment in metamorphosis of spirit
        when time stands silently still
              eternity's angels hold their breath and
                You reach down to hold our hands

      as Your unsuspecting children.
        awestruck, quiet, and full,
            are given the gift of a glimpse
              into the heart of God.

What else is there?

In Jesus' name. Amen.

I, Philip

Phillip said to Him 'Lord, show us the
Father, and we shall be satisfied.' Jesus
said to him, "Have I been with you so long
and yet you do not know Me, Phillip?"
　　　　　　　　　　　　　　　　—John 14:8,9

"In the Bible, my name first appears in Matthew's gospel: 'The names of the twelve apostles are these: first Simon, who is called Peter, and Andrew, his brother; James the son of Zebedee, and John his brother; Philip and Bartholomew; Thomas and Matthew the tax collector; James the son of Alphaeus, and Thaddaeus; Simon the Cananaean, and Judas Iscariot, who betrayed Him.' (Matthew 10:2-4)

"Matthew provides my name and that's it; I am not mentioned again until Mark's gospel. Mark lists me much in the same way Matthew does, with nothing further. Luke's gospel, in keeping with the prior two, summarizes me in one word, my name. In all of them, I am just a name, one of many on a list. I am peripheral to the story, never a participant.

"Then there is John. In John's gospel, I am a person. I have a purpose. I am Philip.

"In his first chapter, John tells us how the early disciples met Jesus. John the Baptist stood with two men when he saw his cousin, Jesus, walking down the road. Upon seeing Him, John the Baptist exclaimed, 'Behold the Lamb of God!' (John 1:29)

"The two men then started following Jesus. When He noticed that they were behind Him, He turned around and asked them what they were seeking. They responded by asking Jesus where He was staying, to which He replied, 'Come and see.' (John 1:39) And they came and saw.

"Later in that first chapter, we learn that Andrew, Peter's brother, was one of the two men that had followed Jesus. John does not tell us, however, that he himself was the second. John was an interesting fellow, you see. Throughout his gospel, John refers to himself as 'the other disciple' or 'the one whom Jesus loved,' never mentioning his own name.

"John mentions my name, but in his gospel I am more than just a name. He writes, 'Jesus decided to go to Galilee. And he found Philip and said to him, "Follow me." (John 1:43)

"I was overjoyed to be found, to know that I was valuable enough for someone to look for me! Jesus found me! I, Philip, believe He was looking specifically for me. He invited *me* to follow Him

"With excitement, I went to see my friend Nathaniel to share my good news. I found him sitting under a fig tree. I said to him, 'We have found Him of whom Moses in the law and also the prophets wrote, Jesus of Nazareth, the son of Joseph.' (John 1:45)

"Nathaniel was a young scholar of the law. He was studying to be a Pharisee. He skeptically asked me, 'Can anything good come out of Nazareth?' (John 1:46)

"I, Philip, said to him, 'Come and see.' (John 1:46) And he came and saw.

"When I brought Nathaniel to Jesus, He immediately recognized him as a good man. He said, 'Behold, an

Israelite indeed, in whom there is no guile!' (John 1:47) As Jesus had noted, Nathaniel was authentic and true.

"Nathaniel said to Him, 'How do you know me?'

"Jesus answered him, 'Before Philip called you, when you were under the fig tree, I saw you.' (John 1:48) Jesus knows you, just as he knew Nathaniel and me. He knows all of us, even before we have names.

"Remember, I was just a name in Matthew's account; I was just a name in Mark's account; I was just a name in Luke's account, but in John's account I am an integral part of Jesus' plan. I brought Nathaniel to Him! *The essence of Christianity is introducing people to Jesus by simply saying, 'Come and see.'*

"I have an indelible memory of a day when Jesus had been preaching on a hillside in Galilee. The account says, 'Lifting up His eyes, then, and seeing that a multitude was coming to Him, Jesus said to Philip, "How are we to buy bread, so that these people may eat?" (John 6:5)

"I was surprised and honored that Jesus turned to me, Philip, for my opinion. Giving my best estimate, I responded, 'Two hundred *denarii* would not buy enough bread for each of them to get a little.' (John 6:7)

"Andrew, who overheard our conversation, offered, 'There is a lad here who has five barley loaves and two fish; but what are they among so many?' (John 1:9)

"Jesus' response to Andrew was, 'Make the people sit down.' (John 6:10) He took the five barley loaves and the two tiny fish. After blessing them, He told us to distribute them to the people. We fed everyone present and filled twelve baskets with the food that was uneaten!

"John's gospel states that there were five thousand in the crowd that day. However, Matthew's account, in all probability, is more accurate. He writes, 'And those who ate were about five thousand men, not counting women and children.' (Matthew 14:21) It is possible that as many as twelve thousand people had been fed! It was a miracle!

"Note that John described the bread specifically as barley bread, which only the poorest of the poor ate. The two small fish in the boy's basket were not the size of the fish that Peter, James and John would have caught on the Sea of Galilee. These were tiny fish, similar to sardines. John's purpose in providing these details is to emphasize that the boy's meal was meager, measly. This literary technique serves to heighten the magnitude of the miracle.

"To me, Philip, the incident on the hillside was a double-miracle. Jesus had thought enough of me to ask for my opinion; I was more than just a name to Him.

"I also recall an occurrence following the celebration at the home of Mary and Martha, after Jesus had raised their brother, Lazarus, from the dead. As news of this miracle spread, a crowd gathered, waving branches of palm trees and calling 'Hosanna! Blessed is He who comes in the name of the Lord!' (John 12:13)

"Some Gentiles, Greeks, to be specific, approached me, and said, 'Sir, we wish to see Jesus.' (John 12:21) Now, Jesus' ministry had always been with the Jews. The arrival of the Greeks signified that it was rapidly expanding.

"Jesus then explained to us that *'kairos,'* God's time, had come. 'The hour has come for the Son of man to be glorified.' (John 12:23) I was present when Jesus spoke those pivotal words. I was an active participant, no longer peripheral. The following day was to be the last supper, and shortly thereafter, His crucifixion, death and ultimate resurrection, Easter.

"Remember, I was just a name in Matthew; I was just a name in Mark; I was just a name in Luke, but in John's account I have a purpose. In John, I am part of the story. I speak up and become engaged. I am portrayed as a philosopher who, by questioning, 'Why?' uncovers the greatest of all theological truths.

"When we were in the Upper Room, Jesus told us that we should not let our hearts be troubled. In our Father's house were many rooms, He explained. He was going away to prepare a place for us. Among the disciples was Thomas, the intellectual, the 'doubter,' as he became known. Thomas never accepted any truth without evidence, proof. Because he did not know where Jesus was going, he feared he wouldn't be able to find Him. He was confused by Jesus' words and questioned Him.

"Jesus responded, 'I am the way, and the truth, and the life; no one comes to the Father, but by me. If you had known me, you would have known my father also; henceforth you know Him and have seen Him.' (John 14: 6,7)

"Not anticipating the theological implications of what His response would be, I, Philip, spoke up and asked, 'Lord, show us the Father, and we shall be satisfied.' (John 14:8)

"He turned to me—unimportant, unclaimed Philip, always listed, but never of interest to anyone until Jesus found me—and said, 'Have I been with you so long, and yet you do not know me, Philip? He who has seen me has seen the Father; how can you say, "Show us the Father?" Do you not believe that I am in the Father and the Father in me? The words that I say to you I do not speak on my own authority; but the Father who dwells in me does His works. Believe me that I am in the Father and the Father in me; or else believe me for the sake of the works themselves.' (John 14: 9-11)

"With these words I began to understand. I felt their import in my heart. I had been with Jesus. I heard His words. I witnessed the lame walk, the blind see, the deaf hear, and the mute sing His praises. I even saw the dead rise to renewed life! All of these works I had seen, yet I never grasped their significance. By posing my incomprehension as a question, I became a vehicle for John to declare in his gospel that this Galilean, this carpenter's son, was the living and true God!

"I believe, beyond a shadow of a doubt, that Jesus was Jehovah; the God of Abraham, Isaac, and Jacob. 'In the beginning was the word, and the word was with God and the word was God. He was in the beginning with God, all things were made through Him, and without Him was not anything made that was made. In Him was life, and the life was the light of men.' (John 1:1-4)

"Jesus was the *logos*, the incarnate. I am totally and absolutely convinced that He was God in the flesh. He came as a human and became like us, so we could become like Him!

"Don't be just a name. Listen to His words. Come to the communion table, which He has prepared for us. Take His broken body. Take his shed blood. Come and see! Come and see that you can be more than just a name. You can become an indispensible disciple as I, Philip, remain to this day."

Amen and amen.

"Listen to the wind, Nicodemus,
   listen to the wind!"

   listen to the children's laughter
       look into the eyes of an aging friend

   lift up the fragile flower
       lean forward your support to lend

   let God take care of you tomorrow
       live like He's the beginning and end

"Listen to the wind, Nicodemus,
   listen to the wind!"

Thank You, Jesus, for whispering to me those
      soft sentences
          showing I'm in process
              of being changed
                  the way you want me to be.

In Jesus' name. Amen.

I, Nicodemus

Now there was a man of the Pharisees, named Nicodemus, a ruler of the Jews. This man came to Jesus by night and said 'Rabbi, we know that you are a teacher come from God, for no one can do these signs that you do, unless God is with him.
—John 3:1-2

"I am Nicodemus, the Pharisee. Matthew, Mark and Luke did not mention me in their gospels. Only John included me.

"John, who wrote the last gospel, was a learned man, a student of theology, poetry and philosophy. As a young man studying the law, he trained with the Pharisees. We knew him and he knew us.

"John knew the secret, because he was a secret disciple. On the night Jesus was dragged before the court of Caiaphas, the young maiden assigned to watch the door detained Peter. Hearing his Galilean accent, she suspected he was one of Jesus' disciples. However, she recognized John as one of the familiar young law students. He was permitted to enter the court because his discipleship was a secret.

"Throughout John's gospel, he writes with the vocabulary and acumen of a lawyer, using terms like 'bear witness' and 'have an advocate.' John understood. That's why he was the disciple to write about me.

"I, Nicodemus, was also a lawyer. In fact, as a Pharisee, I belonged to an elite group of lawyers;

we were distinguished from the others, as our name 'Pharisee,' meaning 'separate,' implies. The task of a Pharisee was to interpret the laws defining good Jewish behavior and expound upon their multiple intentions and applications. Over time, the laws had become increasingly complex and confusing. For example, they specifically stipulated how far a person could walk on the Sabbath. Pharisees were dedicated to deciphering the minutiae of the laws and explaining them to the people. We were the teachers.

"John and I used to talk in the evening about truth, belief and the faith of our fathers. We discussed the prophets of old, who taught that a Messiah was to come and free the people.

"John was a very perceptive person. He knew. He recognized that there was something missing in my life. One day, he told me there was a new teacher among us. Oddly, He was a carpenter's apprentice from Nazareth in Galilee, who had never been schooled, as John and I had been. John told me that even though this teacher was the unlettered son of a carpenter, when He spoke, He commanded divine authority. His listeners hung on His every word.

"I, Nicodemus, became intrigued. I wanted to see this new teacher, but I wanted to do it secretly. Remember, I was a Pharisee. As such, I held standing in the community for being one who knew the law. I could not let it be said that I, Nicodemus, questioned the law and had sought answers from a mere carpenter's apprentice who associated with fishermen. Thus, I went to see the one who would later be called 'rabbi,' at night. The hour was appropriate because nighttime was when we lawyers did our studying.

"In John's gospel, he writes, 'This man came to Jesus by night.' (John 3:2) With these words, John is not referring only to the time of day; he is subtly telling you that I, Nicodemus, who had been lauded for my credentials and knowledge of the law, was still in the dark. Thus, in the dim darkness of my ignorance, I went to Him at night.

"Hesitatingly, I said to Him, 'Rabbi, we know that you are a teacher come from God; for no one can do these signs that you do, unless God is with Him.' (John 3:2)

"This man said to me, a grown adult, 'Truly, truly, I say to you, unless one is born anew, he cannot see the kingdom of God.' (John 3:3)

"Puzzled, I replied 'How can a man be born when he is old? Can he enter a second time into his mother's womb and be born?' (John 3:4)

"Jesus answered, 'Truly, truly I say to you, unless one is born of water and the Spirit, he cannot enter the kingdom of God. That which is born of the flesh is flesh, and that which is born of the Spirit is spirit. Do not marvel that I said to you "You must be born anew." The wind blows where it wills, and you hear the sound of it, but you do not know whence it comes or whither it goes; so it is with every one who is born of the Spirit.' (John 3: 5-8)

"There is a branch of philosophy called epistemology, the study of knowledge, what we know and what we do not know. This carpenter's apprentice said to me, a scholar of philosophy, 'Are you a teacher of Israel, and yet you do not understand this? Truly, truly I say to you, we speak of what we know, and bear witness to what we have seen; but you do not receive our testimony. If

I have told you earthly things and you do not believe, how can you believe if I tell you heavenly things? No one has ascended into heaven but He who descended from heaven, the Son of man. And as Moses lifted up the serpent in the wilderness, so must the Son of man be lifted up, that whoever believes in Him may have eternal life.' (John 3:10-15)

"I walked home that night in the dark, but those days of darkness were gone. John knew. When I first went to Jesus, I was still in the dark of spiritual confusion and uncertainty. But I was on my way to the light.

"While I walked, in my mind I could still hear Him speaking the words 'Truly, truly I say to you . . .' John quoted them in his gospel, employing a literary technique that would later become known as the use of 'double emphatics.' 'Truly, truly' signifies to the reader, as Jesus signified to me, that attention should be paid, that the words to follow would be of immense, eternal importance.

"Under this directive, I carefully pondered everything He had taught me. I mused, for example, on His use of the Greek word *pneuma,* which means both 'wind' and 'spirit.' As the wind blows, so too does the Spirit. One knows not from where the Spirit comes, nor where it goes, only that it is.

"I appear three times in John's gospel, which is not a coincidence. Three, for John, is a holy number. He is telling you of my holy pilgrimage, my spiritual development and emergence into the light of truth.

"My journey had three stages, the first of which I just shared with you. The second stage, as John tells you, was at a meeting of the Pharisees. Tensions were building, as many Jews had begun calling the itinerant preacher 'rabbi.' Jesus' popularity and persuasion were increasing dramatically with each passing day. My colleagues wanted to seize Him and arrest Him.

"One day, certain officials had heard one of Jesus' sermons. Some of them wanted to arrest Him, but no one laid hands on Him. The officers then went back to the chief priests and Pharisees, who said to them, "Why did you not bring Him?" (John 7:44-45)

"The officers answered, "No man ever spoke like this man." (John 7:46)

"Angered, my colleagues began to strategize and organize their trap for Him. At their next meeting, I, Nicodemus, stood up and spoke about the law relative to the Galilean. I had to speak prudently, because my identity as a disciple was a secret, like my friend John's had been. However, my courage was growing in proportion to my commitment to Him. I summoned strength from the Spirit, that '*dunamas*,' of which Jesus spoke, from which you get your word 'dynamite.'

"To the Pharisees, six hundred strong, I said 'Does our law judge a man without first giving him a hearing and learning what he does?' (John 7:51)

"They turned to me and said, 'Are you from Galilee too? Search and you will see that no prophet is to rise from Galilee.' (John 7:52) I didn't respond, but I wanted to say that my life had been changed by that Galilean.

"The third and last time I appear in John's account was on the afternoon of Good Friday. My friend, Joseph of Arimathea, and I prepared the limp, breathless body of Jesus with one hundred pounds of aloe, myrrh and perfume, which I had carried on my back. Joseph's family had dug a granite tomb for Jesus, outside the lower wall of Jerusalem, not far from the place of His crucifixion. We wrapped Him in linen cloths and laid Him in the tomb.

"I, Nicodemus, saw Jesus' dead body. But three days later, that very body was vibrant and alive, the most powerful life the world has ever known. It was Easter!

"The risen Christ transformed me. I stand before you as a witness saying that I, Nicodemus, was spiritually confused and in the dark, but now I live in the light. It is Easter morning every day!"

Amen and amen.

There's a special stirring in the soul
one feels as the Lenten season begins,
which is commensurate with the life
known to be struggling in the earth
as the spring season stretches the days,
after the cold, dull, darkness of winter.

O life of Christ, burst in my being
as even now life breaks loose in ground and bush
pushing aside the hard, half-frozen crust
of winter's temporary encasement of life,
holding beauty prisoner and growth captive
until called forth by resurrection to a new day.

In Jesus' name. Amen.

I, Peter

Simon, Simon, behold the Evil One demanded to have you, that he might sift you like wheat, but I have prayed for you that you faith may not fail; and when you have turned again, strengthens your brethren.
—Luke 22: 31-32

Mark sits at a wooden table writing quickly, as the large Galilean fisherman tells his story. The two men, one young, the other old, share a mutual devotion; their hearts beat with a common cause. The low flame of a small oil lamp softly illuminates Mark's manuscript. He isn't writing in flawless Greek, but he is eagerly and enthusiastically recording for generations yet unborn the experiences of the older man.

The great fisherman from Galilee paces back and forth as he speaks. He pauses now and again to rest his elbows on the windowsill and gaze into the midnight sky. Sometimes, even midsentence, his timbre slowly fades until it is no longer audible. Looking up at the silhouetted disciple, Mark can see his lips moving in silence. Peter slips into conversation with his God as naturally as he breathes. Then he seamlessly resumes his pacing, back and forth across the floor, speaking fluently and thoughtfully.

Peter speaks of the Passover meal of broken bread and a shared cup in the upper room. Mark nods knowingly as he writes, for the room was in the home of his mother. Asleep in his bed, young Mark had been awakened by the sweet sound of men singing a hymn. With a voice that is beginning to break, Peter tells Mark that Jesus and the disciples went to the Mount of Olives after they had finished their supper in the upper room. Jesus said to them, "You will all fall away; for it is written, 'I will strike the shepherd, and the sheep will be scattered.'" (Mark 14:27)

Having heard this, Peter had told Him, "Even though they all fall away, I will not." (Mark 14:29)

In response, Jesus turned to him and said, "Truly I say to you, this very night, before the cock crows twice, you will deny me three times." (Mark 14:30)

Peter's reply had been quick and certain. "If I must die with you, I will not deny you." (Mark 14:31)

At this moment, Peter stops speaking. The silence of the room is shaken by the tragic sobs of one tormented by remorse and regret. For Peter has not forgotten the Mount of Olives . . . or Gethsemane . . . or Calvary. With hot tears scalding his cheeks, he rushes over and grabs his young scribe by the arm saying,

"Don't stop! Keep writing, man!

"I, Peter, boasted that I would never disown him! That claim was stuffed with the innards of a coward! I, Peter, slept in the garden of Gethsemane like a sluggard, when I should have been watching Him, waiting for Him. The others scattered like leaves in a storm. I stayed, but I hid like a rabbit in a thicket.

"I watched them drag Him out of the garden in the dark of night, while just days before, He rode triumphantly through the city gates of Jerusalem in the light of day. Men had saluted Him with palm branches! Women had paved his path with flowers! 'Hosanna!'

they shouted. 'Blessed is He who comes in the name of the Lord!' (Psalm 118:26)

"But that night, where were they? Indeed, where was I? It was easy to be a follower on that first Palm Sunday, singing psalms and shouting praises with the crowd. But in Gethsemane's garden, I, Peter, who had walked toward Him on the waters of Galilee, hid behind a tree, letting those crass centurions take Him.

"I did not even feel the olive branches when they tore my cloak and cut my face till it bled, as I fled from the garden to the court. With every step, my head and heart pounded, coursing with the question, 'Was it supposed to end like this?'

"I reached the courtyard of the high priest, which was crammed with riffraff and rogues. The early morning air bit my bare shoulders. I stepped closer to one of the fires for warmth. In the light of the fire, a maiden, who had been watching the gate, noticed me. She said, 'You also were with the Nazarene, Jesus.' (Mark 14:67)

"I was frightened. The accusing finger of a young girl intimidated me, Peter, who had fought the fierce storms of the Galilean Sea. I quickly denied it, saying, 'I neither know nor understand what you mean.' (Mark 14:68)

"The girl said to those around me, 'This man is one of them.' (Mark 14:69) Again, I denied it.

"The men who had heard the girl recognized my accent and said, 'Certainly you are one of them; for you are a Galilean.' (Mark 14:70) 'You just shuddered when you heard the clink of His chains. You just winced when you heard the guard slap him! Admit it; you know Him.'

"I used language I had not used since I had known

Him, when I worked so hard on the fishing boats of Galilee. It was livid and profane. I sounded like a deranged demon, not a disciple. My vehemence shocked everyone around me, even the vulgar centurions. There was an embarrassing, deafening silence.

"Then, like a trumpet call, came the distant crowing of a cock. I immediately remembered His prophecy and my promise. I broke that promise by openly denying Him three times, just as He had said I would. Through my tear-blurred eyes, I saw Him on the steps. He had heard every searing swearing word, every damned denial. I, Peter, wanted to die.

"Mark, do you want to write about grace? He was bruised and beaten, His faced pelted with spittle. But *He looked at me through the eyes of His heart.* His eyes forgave me. I, Peter, wept like a baby.

"I recalled the words He had spoken to me earlier that evening, 'Satan demanded to have you, that he might sift you like wheat, but I have prayed for you that your faith may not fail; and when you have turned again, strengthen your brethren.' (Luke 22:31,32) I, Peter accepted and embraced His command.

"Record it all, Mark. Let everyone know that we are all bestowed with the grace of His forgiveness. 'Blessed is he who comes in the name of the Lord.'" (Psalm 118:26)

Amen and amen.

Dear God,

When will we learn
   to stop setting the agenda
      and making the rules
         as we go along?

At the end of the day
   we feel and look so puny and pathetic
      exhausted by making a religion
         out of planning our own process
            arranging our personal satisfactions
            accommodating life to suit
               our own hidden agendas.

Help us see that "it works"
   only when we plug into your process
      and pace ourselves by slipping
         into the constancy of faith's
            divine center
   for only there in simple trust
      do we discover
         the unexpected joys with which
            You wish to surprise Your children.

Forgive us for struggling so hard
   to set things up and be in control
      that we miss the point
         of grace*ful* living.

In Jesus' name. Amen.

I, Judas

Then one of the twelve, who was called Judas Iscariot, went to the chief priests and said, 'What will you give me if I deliver Him to you?
—Matthew 26:14,15

"*Judas Iscariot*—my, how the very mention of my name seems to boil up hostility and hatred. 'Judas Iscariot, betrayer of the Son of God.' As soon as my name is mentioned, I can smell the stench of ignominy that has accompanied it for centuries. 'Judas Iscariot, betrayer of the Son of God.'

"I was not so bad, you know, certainly not as bad as some of the others. So, let's take a look, shall we?

"I was a good disciple. I had ability and talent. I was trusted. Christ himself came to me and said, 'Judas, with your keen mind and practicality, I would like you to manage the purse.'

"I, Judas was proud that day. From then on, I stuck my chest out. I was a bit better than the other disciples. As keeper of the purse, I held a superior position. I was respected. My reputation was solid. When Christ said, 'One of you will betray me' they all asked Him, 'Lord, is it I?' No one pointed a finger at me! No, as I said, I was a good disciple.

"I'm not so dreadful, really. The so-called Messiah betrayed *me*. He called me to follow Him! He promised a new kingdom, a new Israel!

"After two or three years of preparation, I expected

that, like a king, He would parade through the gates of Jerusalem with a crown on His head and sit upon the throne of David. There was a parade—He rode into Jerusalem on the back of a mule! Later that week, He received His crown—a crown of thorns!

"The other disciples did not suspect that I, Judas, respected, trustworthy Judas, would call His hand. One night after we had supped, a woman brought an ointment, that expensive ointment. She broke an alabaster jar, spilling the contents onto His feet and wiping them with her hair. It was absurd! I spoke in opposition, saying that we could have traded that ointment for food and clothing for the poor. He had the audacity to contradict me, saying, 'The poor you always have with you, but you do not always have me.' (John 12:8) With those words, I had had all I could take.

"I had to force a change. I had to call His hand. Thus, I went to the high priests. I wanted ninety pieces of silver. They cut it down to sixty. Before I could accept, they cut it further still, to thirty. I could have gotten more. He was the leader of a new subversive movement. Besides, He was a good catch. He was young, strong and healthy, certain to die a slow death. I should have gotten more.

"Shortly thereafter, in the garden of Gethsemane, I planted a kiss of betrayal upon His cheek. It was a rather sweet kiss, really, but it turned sour and disgusting. The Roman soldiers clamored and clanked around Him with their armor and swords. He said, 'Let the scriptures be fulfilled' (Mark 14:49) and left with them without resistance.

"I waited for an angelic host to rain down in armies, splitting the heavens wide, to lift Him up and place Him on the throne of David. The angels did not come. A farce of a trial was followed by His public death. He never had a throne. I, intellectually superior Judas, realized too late that *His* kingdom was one of suffering, surrender and sacrifice. I felt like such a fool. I had been too focused on my own agenda. When the Christ didn't meet my expectations, I forced the hand of God. In the deepest dark of blackness and bitterness, I took my own life.

"I really wasn't so bad. True, I betrayed Him. But Peter denied Him. I was not the only villain, you know. There was a difference between Peter and me, however. After the Christ was brought to the court of the High Priest, He overheard Peter deny Him. He walked out to the courtyard. Peter looked up at Him. He looked at Peter. In that look, Peter saw love, compassion and forgiveness.

"After I kissed Him, I did not see Him look at me with the look that He gave Peter. But I know it was there. From this side of eternity, I have learned that love, compassion and forgiveness are the very essence of the Messiah. This king needed no throne.

"I am Judas Iscariot. Don't look down your long noses of righteousness at me! I did the socially acceptable thing in the act of my betrayal. I went up to Him, put my arms around His shoulders and kissed Him, as was our custom. Oh, how sinister was that kiss! And how superficial was I not to notice His look of love, compassion and forgiveness! But I did the socially acceptable thing.

"If you come to His table and partake of His broken body and shed blood because it is the acceptable thing to do, you are as much a Judas as I. Rather, illuminate your life by His presence. Lift high His cross, so that all will see it and be drawn unto Him. For as He said,

'I, when I am lifted up from the earth, will draw all men to myself.' (John 12:32) 'I have come as light into the world.' (John 12:46) Illuminate others with the light of Christ! Or eliminate him altogether, as I did.

"I, Judas, was a man of promise and potential. As the great Scottish preacher, Dr. James S. Stewart, once wrote, 'The Master's eye, accustomed to reading all kinds of people, detected in Judas the makings of a real apostle. He was a man who had it in him to do splendid service for the Kingdom. Sometimes, indeed, it has been suggested that Jesus gave Judas a place near Himself, simply because it was necessary in God's predestined plan for there to be a traitor in the disciples' band. It cannot be too strongly insisted that any such theory is absurd and irreligious. It turns predestination into fatalism. It is a slander on the providence of God's ordering of the world. It degrades the sacred narrative to the level of solemn play acting.'

"No, Jesus called me, Judas Iscariot, to be His disciple, for the same reason that He called the other eleven. He saw in me a man of noble promise and boundless possibility. No doubt, He also saw the moral contradictions battling for supremacy in my secret soul; light vs. darkness, courage vs. cowardice, self-surrender vs. self-absorption. I was a man of human passions, of such stuff as Jesus fashioned people for sainthood. He hoped to do that with me, you know. You are like me. You have the possibility to illuminate the world. Or, eliminate Him altogether, as I did. Nothing in between will do. He's counting on you to make the right decision. Your destiny hangs in the balance."

Amen and amen.

Grace always calls beyond yesterday
inviting you to uncharted experiences
deepening one's life
stretching one's soul
filling one's heart
calling one to embrace life
as it was meant to be.

To live life as such
with exquisite abandon
is to embody eternity's energy
by extending Easter's experience
into the encounters of today
leading to love unending
giving each a gifted dream for tomorrow.

Only grace could be so surprisingly sweet.

In Jesus' name. Amen.

I, Simon of Cyrene

*And they led Him out to crucify Him. And they
compelled a passerby, Simon of Cyrene, who
was coming in from the country, the father of
Alexander and Rufus, to carry His cross.*
                                              —Mark 15:20-21

*He touched me and O the joy that filled my soul.
Something happened and now I know,
He touched me and made me whole.*

(*He Touched Me*, William J. Gaither)

"Have you ever gotten pulled into something in
which you had neither interest nor investment? This is
the story of my participation in just such an incident.

"I am Simon, a Greek-speaking Jew from Cyrene, an
area west of Egypt, in what is now known as Libya. My
wife Ruth and I had saved our *denarii* for many years
to make a pilgrimage with our two sons, Alexander and
Rufus. We had gone to Jerusalem, to visit its historic
cites and to celebrate Passover, a feast that is rich in
tradition to Jews.

"A strange turn of events that occurred during our
trip leads to my tale this morning. My family and I
had been in Jerusalem for several days. We were very
excited that the Passover feast was fast approaching.
Ruth and I wanted to take a final excursion with our

sons prior to the celebration, because we planned to return to Cyrene immediately afterward. We had planned to spend a day exploring the area surrounding the city. Thus it was that we were 'coming in from the country,' as the text says.

"We were casually enjoying our day when we noticed a commotion near the entrance to the city gates. Not knowing that the situation was initiated by the high priest and the chief priests, we paid little attention to the developing crowd.

"The account tells you that a Roman centurion 'compelled a passerby.' I, Simon, was that passerby. The soldier grabbed me. He insisted that I carry the cross of a criminal who was being marched to the place of His execution, up the Via Dolorosa, to the hilltop just outside the city wall. Under the regulations of the occupational Roman empire in Judea, I was obliged to comply. I was annoyed and angered by this intrusion. My family and I had been minding our own business!

"The sweaty condemned criminal, wearing a purple robe, of all things, was staggering and stumbling under the heavy burden of His cross. The sight of Him disgusted me. What kind of a charade of justice was this?

"From the shouting of the crowd, I gleaned that this pathetic-looking stranger was a carpenter-turned-preacher from Galilee. He had been arrested and obviously tortured. In a weakened state, He found it difficult to keep His footing. Exhausted, He fell again and again. Still furious that our holiday had been interrupted, I swore when I lifted the cross from His tired and bleeding shoulders.

"When I relieved Him of this weight, He touched

me. The touch was not a casual brushing. It was intended and deliberate; a tender touch of gratitude and grace. He gently placed His hand upon my forearm and said, 'Thank you. Thank you, my son. May God bless you and yours.'

"Had it not been for this communicating touch, I would have reluctantly carried His cross to its destination, thrown the damned thing down and walked away—without looking back. That touch had a deep impact on me. From that moment, my attitude changed.

"I, Simon, who had been compelled by the Roman soldier to carry this man's cross, now felt compelled by my own volition to complete my assignment with generosity and respect. I, who would have slammed the cross down and stomped away swearing, instead placed it reverently at His feet. In awe of my own words, I heard myself say, 'I thank *you*, sir. It is *you* who are suffering for *me*.'

"No, I did not walk away. I couldn't. I stood spellbound as they nailed Him to the cross I had carried. I watched Him suffer. Even in His agony and pain, I heard Him pray, 'Father, forgive them for they know not what they do.' (Luke 23:34)

"When that man touched me, He transformed my life. I had been touched by the transcendent. Seeing the change in me influenced my family, too. Years later, my sons were called to leadership in the church.

"In the conclusion of his letter to the Romans, Paul mentions my family. He asks them to 'Greet Rufus, eminent in the Lord, also his mother and mine.' (Romans 16:13)

"Note that in Mark's gospel, he identifies me as 'Simon of Cyrene, father of Alexander and Rufus.'

(Mark 15:21) Generally reticent to use proper names, Mark identifies me specifically and my sons inclusively. Jews normally refer to men by associating them with their father, for example, Barjonah means 'son of Jonah.' But I am introduced in a unique manner— through association with my sons. No doubt, they were well known by Mark's audience, the Gentiles.

"I, Simon of Cyrene, am here with you today to declare that the cross makes you a partner with God. The partnership is a new covenant. It will change you and generations who come after you.

"Carrying His cross was not an interruption; it was my introduction to 'the Lamb of God, who takes away the sin of the world.' (John 1:29) It was the beginning of my spiritual resurrection. Yes, I carried His weight, but He carried my burden."

Amen and amen.

At the cross, at the cross where I first saw the light
And the burden of my life rolled away.
It was there by faith I received my sight
And now am happy all the day.

(*Alas! And Did My Savior Bleed,* Isaac Watts)

Reflection on Friday Called "Good"

Jesus died today
      He died for you and me.
He paid the price, went all the way
      that we at one with God could be.

See the cross upon which He hung
      bold, bare and of rough design.
The angels this day in heaven have sung
      that you and I need not resign.

Because He died, we truly may live
      from this Good Friday on
Yet we must daily our own love give
      that others, though lost, may yet be won.

In Jesus' name. Amen.

I, Barabbas

The governor again said to them, 'which of the two do you want me to release for you?' And they said, 'Barabbas . . . . Then he released for them Barabbas, and having Jesus scourged, delivered Him to be crucified.
—Matthew 27:21,26

It is well past midnight. The people of the village went to their beds hours ago, while it was still raining. The clean freshness of the night air is haunting. A strong steady wind blows black clouds swiftly across the sky, darkening the stars that seem to shimmer and shine more brightly after a heavy rain. The full moon is blanketed with a deep purple haze. The night is awash with a quiet that is almost too quiet. Through the silence one can hear only the last of the rainwater as it drips from the rooftops, trickling down to the stream below the well at the center of the village.

Within this scene, our attention is drawn to the pale light from a little opened window of a room in a house in the center of a narrow street. As we follow the light, we focus on the form of an old man in an ill-kept room. He is seated before an oil lamp, whose flame flickers with each gust of wind whipping up the street.

The old man shivers as he pulls and tugs at his tattered camel-hair robe, in a futile attempt to extract more coverage and warmth from it. But the robe cannot stop his trembling, for as we look closer, we see that he is crying. His heaving body is huddled over a scroll. Tears roll down his cheeks and drop pathetically onto the paper, blurring the ink and smearing the lines.

One might conjecture that a short walk through the quiet streets would lift his spirits. But no, he's tried that. Many were the dark, deserted nights when he paced the streets hearing nothing but the metronomic sound of his own footsteps on the cobblestones, beating out the seconds of his loneliness. Their hollow, haunting sound echoed, then reechoed, through the empty alleyways. Rather, he sits night after night on a hard wooden bench with inadequate light, his eyes riveted to this scroll before him, which reads, *'Surely He has borne our grief and carried our sorrows. Yet, we esteemed Him stricken, smitten by God and afflicted. But He was wounded for our transgressions. He was bruised for our iniquities.'* (Isaiah 53:4,5) The words are from the prophet Isaiah. The old man reading them is Barabbas.

There is a stir behind him. He turns and looks up. One of his drunken cronies stumbles into the room.

"Oh, Calepth," he says, "It's you." Embarrassed, Barabbas tries to inconspicuously hide the scroll with the wide sleeve of his robe.

His cruel friend notices his unease, but teases and taunts him anyway. "Barabbas, you fool, you're at it again. Get rid of those old scrolls! Stop this senseless brooding. Come out with us tomorrow night. You're not that old yet. Your hair may be white, but look at those arms! You're still strong and vigorous. You've got spirit left, man! Why not enjoy some excitement instead of rotting in this tiny room?" With a boorish push, Calepth shoves Barabbas' arm across the scroll, knocking it to the floor in a heap.

"Calepth, sit down," he says, "I must talk to someone." Calepth slumps heavily into an old chair. The liquor has made his eyelids turn to lead; his head sags sleepily.

Not dissuaded, Barabbas goes on, relieved that he finally has someone, anyone, to talk to.

"I am Barabbas, the infamous Barabbas. You remember . . . I was freed on the day I was to be crucified, at Pilate's farce of a trial. That's right, Calepth, I am *that* Barabbas. But there is more to me than history knows.

"Have you and the other rascals ever wondered why I could read and write, while you could not? Have you ever noticed anything peculiar about my name? Have you, Calepth?" The head of Calepth shakes a slow negative reply.

"My name 'Bar-rabbas' means 'son of the rabbis.' 'Bar' means 'son;' 'rabbas' means 'of the rabbis.' You see, Calepth, at the time of the insurrection, I was a student of the Torah in the synagogue. I despised the Roman occupiers, so I aided the subversives, the Zealots. I plotted, robbed and murdered for the cause of freedom.

"Eventually, I was arrested and spent three years in a dungeon, smelling the stench of Roman food. They fed me pig entrails and other repulsive things that are disgusting and offensive to Jews. Finally, I was forced to eat them or die.

"I am Barabbas, son of the rabbis. I know this scroll line by line, Calepth. I know the law and the prophets. I can quote Isaiah, and I know the one of whom Isaiah writes."

The memories wrench his heart and hammer his head, causing it to throb and ache. He recalls standing on the white marble floor of the court with his eyes blinking in the sunlight on that bright April morning— the first light he had seen in three years. The crowd's attention was entirely focused on the other condemned prisoner, who was standing beside him.

"When I glanced at Him, I saw an innocent face and kind eyes. I wondered what He could have done, to be on trial like me. Was He too a thief and a murderer, a political subversive, in opposition to the occupying armies of Caesar? Then I learned that He was called Jesus. He was a Nazarene, a carpenter's son. He claimed to be the King of the Jews, the promised Messiah, the Savior of the world.

"I thought to myself, 'That's the reason; the man is a religious fanatic, a lunatic. No wonder He's on trial.' But I observed the stature and poise of the man. Clothed in purple, He held his head high . . . like a king.

"In keeping with the custom of the day, during the Passover feast Pilate asked the crowd which prisoner they would like to be released.

"Calepth, though the account doesn't record it, when the Nazarene saw the hatred in the eyes of the crowd, His eyes filled with tears. Their ugly wretched faces surged forward like a giant wave in an angry sea. They shouted, 'Crucify Him! Crucify Him!' Their cries were deafening. Seconds before His voice was obliterated, He turned his head to Pilate. Softly but emphatically He said, 'Let Barabbas go.' Pilate didn't hear Him. No one in the court heard Him. No one heard Him but me. I was astonished.

"Trying to save the time and expense of a crucifixion, they attempted to beat Him and scourge Him to death. When their efforts failed, they marched Him to Golgotha. I, Barabbas, followed from a safe distance, hiding like a coward. I saw the nails pierce His hands and feet. I heard the sickening thud when His cross was dropped into a freshly dug hole. Hellish flies ate the clotted blood from His wounds. He agonized and twisted in pain, until the muscles of His shoulders stood out like great knots. He cried out, 'My God, my God, why hast thou forsaken me?' (Matthew 27:46)

"It was for me, Calepth, it was all for me! I should have been hanging there, but He went in my place. I, Barabbas, never even took the time to thank Him!

"I, Barabbas, was freed; Jesus, the Christ, went to His death. I, Barabbas was a coward! I, Barabbas, was a scholar of the prophets, yet I failed to connect the words of Isaiah to that son of a carpenter. I bear the scar of a sinner; I have been trying to heal it, to no avail, these many nights and years hence."

His voice trails into the darkness as a final gust of wind sweeps up the street through the little opened window, snuffing out the feeble lamplight.

Thus, we leave the scene, but the Savior remains. Now, you are Barabbas. Christ hung there for you. He died for you. His broken body and his shed blood were for your sins and mine.

Have we been standing where Barabbas stood, astonished that someone could love us enough to lay down His life for us? Have we been cowards, lacking conviction and commitment? Have we neglected to thank Him?

The existential moment of decision confronts us now, as it did Barabbas on that morning long ago. Will we leave our safe hiding places and openly walk with Him up that hill called Golgotha? Will we kneel before the cross and say with absolute abandonment, "Jesus, You died for me, now I want to live for You?" Will we do it?

Let us pray.

Amen and amen.

We met in early spring one day
in the garden's deepest place
where I had quietly gone to pray
there I saw the risen Master's face.

He turned and looked at me
lifting me to His side
He gave me hope and strength, you see
when He put power and peace inside.

Sweet is solitude's quiet pain
by which your heart is emptied and freed
For you realize He is your only gain
as you become all He wants you to be.

In Jesus' name. Amen.

I, Mary Magdalene

"Now on the first day of the week, Mary Magdalene came to the tomb early, while it was still dark."
—John 20:1

"My name is Mary, the Magdalene. There are varying historical accounts of my life and my relationship with Jesus, but most of them are erroneous and distorted.

"My birthplace is the village of Magdala. Magdala is four miles north of the city of Tiberias and seven miles south of the village of Capernaum, the northwest corner of the Sea of Galilee. In the beginning of the first century, Magdala was a flourishing fishing village. Its residents were prosperous and privileged.

"I belonged to a group of women of means, who pooled our resources to support a young Galilean preacher and His disciples. Having heard some of His teachings, we were drawn to His movement of reform and renewal. He spoke of hope and wholeness.

"On a personal level, I followed Him because of a condition that had troubled me for many years. I suffered from depression, a mental illness. My days were dark and dry as dust. My nights were sleepless and sorrowful.

"The disciple Luke was a doctor. Some scholars have conjectured that Luke's interest in Jesus' healings prompted him to research and document His life. Luke introduces me in his gospel as 'Mary, called Magdalene, from whom seven demons had gone out.' (Luke 8:2)

In ancient times, 'demons' and 'evil spirits' were the nomenclature for mental illness. Luke understood the severity of my affliction. 'Seven' in biblical literature is a complete, all-encompassing number. Dr. Luke is telling you that I was an emotional and physical wreck. My depression was as bad as it could get.

"Perhaps you recall the Gerasenes demoniac. Evil spirits possessed him too, causing him to scream and convulse violently. While I could empathize with the depth of his disorder, the demons that seized control of my life did not affect me outwardly. Rather, they hurt me inwardly. I was hopelessly depressed.

"I had heard about the ministry of Jesus. He had impacted the lives of people all along the shoreline of the Galilean sea. People reported feeling cleansed and empowered after seeing Him. The deaf could hear. The blind could see. The mute could sing songs. The lame could dance in exultation for the first time in their lives. Even the dead were raised!

"I wanted to tell Jesus about the sorrows that were burdening me. Until I had heard of Him, hope was lost for me. Countless healers had tried to help me, with no positive outcome. I wanted to meet the one becoming known as the 'Great Physician.'

"Jesus healed me. He gave my life back to me. For that, I loved Him. I was devoted to Him.

> Thank You for letting me
> celebrate who I hoped to be
> but could not become
> without the care
> and concern
> of a loving friend like You.

You are my miracle
bringing back to hope
my dreams of yesterday
long lost in the living of today
buried in the detail of daily duty.

Thank You for loving me to life
by touching my trembling potential
which others had never known or cared to know
hidden safely in my heart by You
until the moment when You would come.

Free me
Unbind me
Set me loose like Lazarus
Calling me out of my death
to Your vital and abundant life.

"When Jesus taught, I could almost finish His sentences. Although I knew nothing about theology at that time, our relationship was one of spiritual brilliance.

"I, Mary Magdalene, am probably best known for having stood at the cross with His mother and John, His beloved disciple. We helplessly watched the One, who had brought relief and comfort to so many, suffer in agony. Even in His pain, He thought of others. The thief hanging on the cross next to Jesus asked for forgiveness and received it. He secured the welfare of His mother by asking John to be like a son to her, and she, like a mother to him.

"I heard Him speak His last words, 'Father, into thy hands I commend my spirit.' (Luke 23:46) I cannot express how it felt to watch Him die. He was taken down from the cross, laid in a tomb and covered with a linen cloth.

"On the third day after His death, I went to the tomb in the early morning. It was still dark. The old gnarled trees were casting ugly shadows. I felt somewhat frightened and very alone.

"I approached the tomb, and found that it was open. A transcendent light emanated from it. The stone sealing the entrance had been rolled away. As quickly as I could, I ran to the disciples and told them, 'They have taken the Lord out of the tomb, and I do not know where they have laid him.' (John 20:2)

"Peter and John immediately started running toward the tomb. John, being much younger than Peter, arrived first. He did not go in, but stood outside in wonder. When Peter arrived, he went straightaway into the tomb. He found it empty; the linen cloth was laying as it was when we had covered Him. Peter walked out dismayed. Then John went in. He observed the empty tomb and the linen cloth with spiritual perception. In his gospel, John uses the Greek word *theorei,* which means 'he saw and believed.'

"Peter and John left, but I remained, completely distressed and downhearted. I could sense the return of the bad feelings that had once troubled me.

"I heard someone moving behind me. Thinking it was the gardener, I said, 'Tell me where you have laid Him, and I will carry Him away.' (John 20:15)

"The response I heard was, 'Mary.' (John 20:16) The voice had the tender tone Jesus always used, whenever He spoke my name. The way He said my name told me I was eternally loved. He had been the spiritual love of my life.

"I turned around. With abandonment and joy, I knelt before Him, exclaiming, *'Rab-boni!'* (John 20:16) which means 'teacher' in Hebrew.

"He said to me, 'Go to my brethren and say to them, I am ascending to my Father and your Father, to my God and your God.' (John 20:17)

"As quickly as I could, I went to the disciples, telling them, 'I have seen the Lord.' (John 20:18) Then I delivered His message, as He had bidden me to do.

"The word 'apostle' is a derivative of the Greek word *aspostoli,* which means 'the one who is sent.' In a literal sense, I was the first apostle. I was the first to be given the command, 'Go tell my brethren.' I was the first, before any of the men, to proclaim His resurrected life. I would later be called *apostolio apostolia,* 'apostle to the apostles!'"

Amen and amen.

Thank You, Lord, for a promise-piled heart
that daringly affirms that all I've ever

believed
hoped
anticipated
imagined
expected
conceived
wondered
dreamed

is
possible
when I yield
with
abandoned
faith
in
You.

In Jesus' name. Amen.

I, Thomas

*Now Thomas, one of the twelve, called the
twin, was not with them when Jesus came.*
—John 20: 24

"My name is Thomas. I am often referred to as
'Doubting Thomas.' I, Thomas, was dubbed and
designated a doubter because I was exceedingly
curious, always asking, 'Why?' I needed a reason, a
rationale. The philosopher René Descartes would
later use doubt as a method for proving authenticity.
Descartes doubted everything, except the obvious fact
that he was thinking. He would famously say, *Cogito
ergo sum,* which in Latin means, 'I think, therefore I
am.' Like Descartes, I demanded proof before I could
believe. To have conviction, I needed to be convinced.

"Less commonly, I am called 'Didymus,' which
means 'the twin,' in Greek. Joses, who is thought to be
one of Jesus' brothers, is mentioned in the gospels of
Matthew and Mark. A local tradition of eastern Syria
suggests that I was the twin of Joses, which would have
made me a brother of Jesus too. However, we all can be
part of Jesus' family, because, as He said, 'My mother
and brothers are those who hear the word of God and
do it.' (Luke 8:21)

"Only my name is mentioned in the gospels of
Matthew, Mark and Luke. But John provides several
incidents in which I, Thomas, play a pivotal role.

"Following the death of Lazarus, Jesus announced

that He was going to visit his family, in Bethany of Judea, which is adjacent to Jerusalem, from whence we had recently returned. We disciples then said to Him, 'Rabbi, the Jews were but now seeking to stone You, and You are going there again?' (John 11:8)

"Though I was a doubter, I was brave. I, Thomas, in my youthful courage, said, 'Let us all go, that we may die with Him.' (John 11:16)

"Another incident occurred near the end of our Lord's earthly ministry. He said to us in the upper room, 'Let not your hearts be troubled. Believe in God; believe also in me. In my Father's house are many rooms; if it were not so, would I have told you that I go to prepare a place for you? And when I go and prepare a place for you, I will come again and will take you to myself, that where I am you may be also. And you know the way where I am going.' (John 14:1-4)

"With each word He had spoken, I became more puzzled and frustrated. I blurted out, 'Lord, we do not know where you are going; how can we know the way?' (John 14:5)

"Jesus replied, 'I am the way, and the truth, and the life; no one comes to the Father, but by me. If you had known me, you would have known my Father also; henceforth you know Him and have seen Him.' (John 14:6,7)

"That night, our worst fears became reality. Jesus was arrested and tortured. The following morning, He was nailed to a cross in Golgotha, outside the city of Jerusalem. I, Thomas, who had been brave and bold, stood in the shadows and watched Him die.

"After His death, I isolated myself from everyone.

I had nothing to say. I wanted to immerse myself in my own thoughts.

"Three days later, the disciples went to His tomb, after Mary Magdalene had reported that it was empty. That night, the first Easter night, the disciples were sitting in the upper room, with the door closed and locked, for fear of the Jews. Jesus appeared to them, saying, 'Peace be with you.' (John 20:19)

"Still nursing my sadness in solitude, I was missing when He came. The disciples later told me, 'We have seen the Lord.' (John 20:25)

"In my disbelief, I replied, 'Unless I see in His hands the print of the nails, and place my finger in the mark of the nails, and place my hand in His side, I will not believe.' (John 20:25)

"Eight days later, on the following Sunday, I was with the disciples in the upper room. Again, fearing the Jews, the door was closed and locked. Suddenly, He was standing before us. Walking directly to me, He said, 'Put your finger here, and see my hands; and put out your hand, and place it in my side; do not be faithless, but believing.' (John 20:27)

"I exclaimed, 'My Lord and my God,' which would later become one of the most convincing and cogent declarations of faith in the New Testament. Because of His presence, I was absolutely certain that Jesus was God incarnate. He knew my needs and struggles, and responded to them. He knows the needs and struggles of all of you, loving each of you as though you are the only one He has to love.

"Yes, I played a part in several of the most significant incidents in John's gospel. Never doubt that you, and all the incidents in *your* life, are significant to Him. Never forget that you are a member of His family, whenever you 'hear the word of God and do it.' (Luke 8:21)

"There is one final moment that I would like to share with you. My story would not be complete without it. John writes 'Jesus revealed Himself again to the disciples by the Sea of Tiberius; and he revealed Himself in this way. Simon Peter, Thomas called the Twin, Nathaniel of Cana in Galilee, the sons of Zebedee, and two others of His disciples were together.' (John 21:1)

"You see, I had learned my lesson! I was present when He came! Don't be missing when He comes, like I was on the night of that first Easter. On the following Sabbath evening, the disciples and I were gathered in the upper room, just as you are gathered in this sanctuary today. Remember Jesus' words, 'For where two or three are gathered in my name, there am I in the midst of them.' (Matthew 18:20) Don't be missing, because you will miss Him. I, Thomas, had needed proof. Now I know beyond the shadow of a doubt. I believe!"

"My Lord and my God!"

Amen and amen.

I do not cease to give thanks for you, remembering you in my prayers, that the God of our Lord Jesus Christ, the Father of glory, may give you a spirit of wisdom and revelation in the knowledge of Him, having the eyes of your hearts enlightened, *that you may know what is the hope to which He has called you, what are the riches of His glorious inheritance in the saints.* (Ephesians 1:16-18)

It is all a matter of seeing with the heart!

Afterword

I could not conclude this book without mentioning another professor, Rev. Dr. Theophilus Mills Taylor. He was installed as occupant of the John McNaugher Chair of New Testament Literature and Exegesis at Pittsburgh Theological Seminary in 1941. In 1958, the PCUSA and the United Presbyterian Church of North America united to form the Presbyterian Church of America, the largest Presbyterian denomination in the country. Dr. Taylor was elected the first moderator of the new General Assembly, where he was honored for his leadership and guidance. He was a gentleman of distinction and a scholar of learning, who carried himself in a manner that commanded respect.

The faculty of the Pittsburgh Seminary held us to the highest standard of excellence in whatever discipline we were studying. Dr. Taylor was an effective and exacting instructor in New Testament Greek. Although he was not part of the Homiletics Department per se, when it was his turn to preach at the chapel services, he provided a revered example.

I will never forget the time when Taylor was the unannounced critic of the two student preachers for the day. (There were always two students carrying out their homiletically assigned duties on such a day.) After they had delivered their sermons, Dr. Taylor walked to the front of the chapel with their manuscripts in his hands. He turned to face the entire student body and the faculty. Laying down both manuscripts, he gently said, "There will be no criticism today, because I have not heard any preaching. Please rise for the benediction."

No one moved. We could not believe what we had heard. Finally, we slowly rose to our feet and he gave the benediction. We left the chapel that day in silence. Thank goodness no one remembers who had "preached" on that occasion. His response shocked it out of our memories.

I share this experience to provide an example of what Dr. Kelley meant in the Foreword, where he wrote, "When the experience at last concluded, you dusted yourself off, having been duly humbled, found comfort furnished by fellow students still awaiting their own ordeal, and moved on."

In those years of preparation, the expectations were high for all of us to be the very best, for which I am profoundly appreciative.

About the Author

Dr. Robert L. Veon has served churches in Arkansas, Pennsylvania, New Jersey, Ohio, Connecticut and Maine.

The Presbytery of Southern New England honored him for fifty years of gospel ministry, at their meeting at Yale University Divinity School in New Haven, Connecticut in 2012. The United States Marine Corps selected him as "Outstanding Spokesman of the Faith" at Camp Quantico, Virginia in 1981. He was a Visiting Fellow at Princeton Theological Seminary in New Jersey and a Visiting Scholar at Union Theological Seminary in New York City.

He holds a BA and a DD from Westminster College in Pennsylvania and an MDiv and a DMin from Pittsburgh Theological Seminary. He attended the University of Edinburgh, Scotland, for a year of post-graduate studies. He has returned to Scotland, Europe and Israel a number of times on study trips. He is currently working toward an MS in Psychology at Husson University.

Dr. Veon and his wife, Susan Jean Michel-Veon, moved to Maine seventeen years ago, when he retired from parish assignments. They have named their home nestled in the woods and on a lake, "Kairos Cove." In "retirement," his passions remain teaching, preaching and writing.

After moving to Maine, Veon was hired as the Athletic Director for Greenville High School. He has taught Ethics, Critical Thinking, Human Behavior in Contemporary Film, and World Religions at Beal College in Bangor and at Kennebec Valley Community College in Fairfield. Twice in the last decade, Veon was nominated by his students and subsequently elected for inclusion in *Who's Who among American Teachers*.

He supplied the pulpit at the Jackman Congregational Church for a year or so. For the last ten years, he has conducted worship and preached at the Union Church UCC in Greenville and the Rockwood Chapel.

Dr. Veon authored a collection of "prayer-poems," *Living on the Growing Edge*, in 1986. It is slated for rerelease. He is currently working on a second volume of poetry, which will be published in 2014.

I went to the woods because I wished to live deliberately. I wished to front only the essential facts of life and see if I could not learn what it had to teach and not, when I came to die, discover that I had not lived.

(*Walden*, Henry David Thoreau)